My Life's Ride to the "Bar J Chuckwagon"

Written by Babe Humphrey with Bob Christensen

Publisher:
Babe Humphrey
Bar J Chuckwagon
4200 Bar J Road
Wilson, WY 83014

ISBN 978-0-578-05895-5

Layout and Book Design
Josh Winward
Syracuse, Utah

Cover Design
Josh Winward
Syracuse, Utah

Printing by Alexander's Print Advantage
Lindon, Utah

First Edition
Printed June 2010

Dedication

This book is dedicated to my wife, Martha, my five children, and all those who have helped me achieve my dream of owning "The Bar J".

I'm thankful for Martha's patience with me as I pushed our wedding vows to the limit chasing rainbows all over the country trying to sing songs for a living. Most of the events in this book happened during what should have been our "stay at home, raise our family time." Somehow we all survived my dream chasin' years.

I'm so proud of our three girls for surviving all this and how they have made it to adulthood and who they are today. I'm proud of our boys and their natural talent. How they stepped in and ran the place without much teaching from me. I think my dream became their dream and they do so well what I used to do. Thanks for taking over. "The Bar J" would not be, without you!

Carry on!

I love you all
Babe

Forward

This is the story of Babe Humphrey who from an early age knew that he wanted to be an entertainer. He had an ear for music and at age nine or ten started playing on an old guitar borrowed from a neighbor. His mom taught him three chords and from that he taught himself to play. Though he can't read a note of music he was able to hear harmony and soon realized that by changing the melody, the bass and the harmony around from top to bottom he could give a song a whole new sound. He was smart enough to know what people liked and he knew they were intrigued by harmony. He developed a triple yodel that was very popular and landed him and his two buddies on the Grand Ole Opry in Nashville, Tennessee. Though he wanted to be an entertainer he didn't want the travel and barnstorming that went with it. He found a better way and arranged for his audiences to come to him. In Nashville they told him it couldn't be done but he proved that it could.

His musical career began in elementary school where he won the first talent contest he ever entered and later when he arranged a guitar duet with a friend to win another contest. Though music was a big thing in his life he also excelled in sports and enjoyed High School athletics and other activities that other teenagers were involved with.

He joined the Marines just out of High School and soon organized a band and was entertaining the troops in Korea. When his enlistment was up he left the service and returned to Colorado Springs and got started in the Chuck Wagon Supper business.

A year or two later along with two friends he rode 3100 miles across the country on horseback covering about thirty one miles a day and entertaining each night to raise funds for the Damon Runyan Cancer Fund.

The next ten years were spent at The Flying W Chuchwagon which he managed while he helped it to expand. Sandwiched in this period was two USO tours, one to the Far East military installations and the second to Viet Nam and Thailand.

He then landed in Jackson Hole, Wyoming where he built "The Bar-J Chuckwagon" which has been feeding and entertaining guests from all over the world for over thirty years. The first time many folks go to the Jackson Hole area is to see the Tetons. The subsequent trips are to visit "The Bar J Chuck Wagon."

Babe is retired now from the entertaining side of The Bar-J but left it in the capable hands of his two sons Scott and Bryan who perform nightly Memorial Day through the end of September and then take the show on the road to select locations during the off season.

Babe is still active in the business and now lives with his wife of over 55 years, Martha, in Las Vegas, Nevada in the winter months, they then drive their motor home to Jackson for the summer.

He still enjoys song writing and performing and spends time arranging music on his guitar. He has recorded a CD of oral recitations that he used through the years on the shows which includes some cowboy poetry.

He is looking forward to being in Jackson for the summer so he can help bring along the next generation of Humphrey entertainers, his talented grandsons and grand-daughters.

He also enjoys a round of golf every chance he gets especially with his family and old friends.

Many years ago, soon after I had met Babe, he ask me if I would be interested in being on the show as he was always experiencing some turnover as performers came and went. I told him I didn't sing or play an instrument but he told me not to worry as he could teach me. He pointed out that maybe I could play a bass. I was flattered but felt that I knew my limitations so I just laughed it off and the conversation went in a different direction.

After helping Babe write his life's story and learning of his many accomplishments and the things he has done I have had second thoughts about doubting his ability to teach me these things. In other words, "Now, I believe."

Babe has had an amazing life and the many lessons he has learned he passes on in this book.

I hope you will enjoy reading this book as much as I have enjoyed helping Babe write it. He has indeed had a remarkable ride to The Bar J.

Bob Christensen
Syracuse, Utah

Introduction

It seems that every time I get to talking with folks about growing up and the events that have shaped my life over the years, my career, my family, and my faith in God, somebody says, "You ought to write a book."

This is what Bob Christensen said while we ate breakfast at Jeremiah's Restaurant on West 12th Street in Ogden, Utah, one December morning in 2007.

"Maybe I should, but I would need some help getting it organized and written down." I thought out loud.

Bob thought about it and told me, "Babe, if you will tell me the story, I will help you write it."

I had met Bob twenty years earlier at the National Cowboy Poetry Gathering in Elko, Nevada, where we both performed during the week of the Gathering. We became friends, and I invited him to come up to "The Bar-J Chuckwagon" in Jackson Hole, Wyoming a time or two to entertain our friends and customers with some cowboy poetry. In 1992, the summer after he retired from the Pillsbury Company, he spent the whole summer with us doing twenty minutes of poetry for the dinner crowd as they waited for us to serve them.

By the time I had finished my pork chop at breakfast that morning, Bob and I had decided to write this story. I then racked my brain and wrote some notes so we could document the seventy-five years of my life.

Now, I consider every person I have ever met as having had an influence on who I am. All of the things that have happened in my life have helped mold me into who I am now. Some folks I have spent more time with than with others. My ride through life has brought me into contact with a considerable number of people and taken me to many places. I have participated in life to the fullest and gained much experience. Every time I rub shoulders with someone, some of them rubs off on me.

I guess it's fair to say that much of who I am I owe to my ancestors. Not only physical characteristics but a good work ethic, and I hope a good character. My musical talent can be attributed to ancestors on both sides of the family as several of them were musically inclined.

Babe Humphrey, Painting by Bob Loper

Chapter One

ANCESTORS

The turn of the twentieth century found all of my grandparents living in southern Missouri. My maternal grandparents, Albert and Amanda Williams, came from this part of Missouri. At least my grandfather did. His obituary states that he was born in Meta, Missouri, which is just two counties west of where the Humphreys hail from. He was a farmer and a blacksmith and an extraordinary fiddle player. I wish I knew the story of how they came west, but I have never heard it. I do know that Grandma Williams died in child birth.

My paternal grandparents, Albert and Mertie Humphrey, were shown on the 1900 census as living in

Upper Left- Mr. and Mrs. Robert
Humphrey
(Babe's Great-Grandparents)

Upper Right- Delbert and Bertha
Humphrey
(Babe's Parents)

Bottom Left- Albert and Mertie
Humphrey
(Babe's Grandparents)

Goldsberry, Howell County, Missouri. In a letter I have written by their daughter, Bertha, she tells how they left Missouri in 1907 to come west. I include this letter here as it provides insight into the difficulties that Albert and Mertie faced coming to Colorado.

I was born in and lived in Mountain View, Missouri, until I was 16. The water was very poor, and there was a lot of malaria with chills and fever. Our family of nine fought it every winter. In March of 1907, my father sold all of the farm implements. He rigged up two good covered wagons with over-juts* on each and two good teams (or spans) of mules. He loaded his family of nine into the wagons and headed west. My youngest brother was three months old.

To make a long story short, we made it to Midway, Missouri, a coal mining town a short way out of Pittsburg, Kansas. My father and my 14-year-old brother hauled coal with our wagon and mules for four dollars a day each. They worked at this for six weeks to get money to continue westward.

On May 15th, we loaded up again and headed for Pikes Peak. We always tried to camp at night where we could get milk and water. Some places in Kansas we had to buy water. Some places would not even sell us water, and we had to go on. The trip went fine until my mother developed typhoid fever. We had to lay over in a little town in Kansas to get a doctor for her. As soon as she was able to travel, we journeyed on.

How well I remember seeing Pikes Peak for miles and miles and days before we reached our destination. We arrived at Rocky Ford, Colorado on June 16th and settled on a large ranch three miles east of town. Doctor Fenton owned the ranch. My uncle and his family already lived on the ranch, having come west the year before.

We lived in two tents for most of the summer, and my father, two of my sisters, Grover, a boy my folks raised, and I worked the farm all summer. We thinned sugar beets, hoed cantaloupe, made crates under the tents, and then picked and packed the cantaloupe. The most difficult work for us girls was the harvesting of the sugar beets, but we worked hard. We didn't know anything else. After the harvest was over, we moved to Rocky Ford.

In July, my father and uncle went up to Oryland country and filed homestead claims, and in November they went back to build two room shacks on the land. The homesteads were located sixty miles east of

Colorado Springs, about fifteen miles from Ramah. Our mail was on a star route and was delivered every other day by horse and carriage. Our place was the A.M. Humphrey homestead. Perhaps some of the homesteaders remember what it was like. A family of nine in two 14 X 14 foot rooms with no other buildings of any kind.

We traveled to our new home in January of 1908 with two mule teams, two cows, a dozen chickens, and, of course, our shepherd dog that we had brought from Missouri. The dog walked the entire journey. He refused to ride in the wagons.

We had no water. We had to haul our water in large barrels from three miles away for over a year. The chickens roosted under the house, and we fixed tents for cows and mules. Our homestead shanty was tar-roofed with brown building paper, then tar paper and dirt. The inside was lined with brown building paper.

During the next years, homesteaders settled on every quarter section of land. Soon there was a schoolhouse built in which we held Sunday school and church. A minister came from Colorado Springs. We had parties almost every week, which young and old enjoyed. Our pride and joy was our organ, and on long winter

evenings, after the chores were done and the dishes were washed, we gathered around the organ and sang songs of those days. Songs like Baggage Coach Ahead, My Wandering Boy, Young Charlotte, and *Wreck of The Old '97. Those were the good old days.*
~ *Bertha Humphrey*

*I think over-juts were extensions of the wagon to cover both the front and the rear. They provided more shade and more protection from rain for the folks riding in the wagon.

Albert Humphrey's Fair-Veiw Farm Circa 1917 about 15 miles south of Simla, Co

Chapter Two

THE EARLY LIFE

Things went well for the homesteaders at Fairview Farms, as Granddad had named their place, in Colorado. Over the next ten years, Albert and Mertie's family grew as their children married and started families of their own.

Albert made improvements to his farm, such as building a barn, a potato cellar, a shed, and other outbuildings. Albert was quite a horse guy. He did blacksmith work and bartered with neighboring farms, taking care of their horses in exchange for food.

And then tragedy struck. Three of Albert and Mertie's daughters had married, and one sister, my dad Delbert, and his brother Virgil still lived at home. One morning Granddad and his son-in-law, B.W. Backus, Bertha's husband, had an argument. The argument turned into a fight, and Granddad prevailed. Later in the day, as Granddad visited with a neighbor, Backus shot him in the back from a distance of sixty feet. Backus then made sure that Granddad was dead by bludgeoning him with a crowbar. He filled his pockets with ammunition and fled.

Backus had run to Kiowa County from Elbert County, where the murder took place, and was found there hiding in the middle of a herd of cattle. He was soon apprehended by a Sheriff's posse and stood trial. He pled not guilty by reason of insanity. He was committed to the state mental hospital in Pueblo, Colorado. He was never released and eventually died in that asylum. Grandpa Humphrey was buried in the graveyard in eastern Colorado by his homestead. Bertha divorced Backus shortly after the incident and never saw him again.

A few months after Granddad's death, Grandmother Mertie decided that she couldn't run the farm by herself and sold it. She held a public auction, selling off all the farm equipment and livestock.

RANCHER SHOT AND KILLED BY SON-IN-LAW YESTERDAY

Posse Captures Slayer Yesterday Afternoon After Long Chase Thru Elbert County

A. M. Humphrey, aged 48 years, was shot and instantly killed at the Backus ranch, 12 miles southeast of Simla, yesterday morning by his son-in-law, H. W. Backus, who is said to have been suffering from an attack of insanity at the time of the shooting. Backus escaped immediately afterwards but was surrounded yesterday afternoon by a posse from Simla and placed under arrest. He now is in jail at Madison.

Deputy District Attorney Jack Carruthers left last night for Elbert county to hold an inquest upon the death and to conduct the preliminary hearing of Backus.

Mr. Humphrey has lived near Simla for the last 10 years. He is survived by his wife, four daughters, Mrs. George W. Gordon; 610 South Nevada avenue, of this city; Mrs. Robison, Mrs. Backus, an unmarried daughter living near Simla and two small sons,

Public Sale

As I am leaving the farm I will sell at public auction at my place 10 miles south and 3 east of Simla, 2½ miles west of Eagle Bluff school house, 2 miles north and 1½ east of Holt Ranch, on

THURSDAY, FEBRUARY 22nd

Promptly at 10 A. M., the Following Property, To-Wit:

16 HEAD OF LIVESTOCK

HORSES

Bay horse smooth mouth 1250
Grey horse smooth mouth 1300
Grey mare smooth mouth 1100
Black mare 7 yr old wt 1200
Sorrel saddle pony 4 yr old

IMPLEMENTS

Deering grain binder 8-ft and trucks
3-section harrow
David Bradled lister 14-inch
John Deere 2-row weeder
Little Jap 6-shovel cultivator
Hay rake
Disc harrow
Superior grain drill
2 sets of work harness
Bean cutter
3¼-in wagon and rack

Mitchel wagon
Blacksmith tools
Grindstone
Scoop shovel
Buggy
Hog wire

Household Goods

Writing desk
Bed and springs
Sanitary cot
Dresser
Organ
2 stand tables
Rocking chair
Heating stove
6-hole range with resevoir
Cupboard
Commode
Kitchen cabinet
Daisy churn
Washing machine
Wringer
Improved American separator
Other articles to numerous to mention

CATTLE

Brindle cow giving milk
Red cow 7 yr old fresh soon
Red cow 6 yr old giving milk
Red cow 7 yr old giving milk
Spotted heifer 3 yr fresh soon
White-faced heifer 2 yr old fresh soon
2 red yearling heifers

HOGS

Sow wt 300 lb
2 shoats 80 and 100 lb

CHICKENS

3 dozen R. I. hens
1 dozen mixed hens

FREE LUNCH   **BRING CUPS**

TERMS:—Sums of $10 and under cash. Sums over $10 a credit of 9 months time at 10 per cent interest on bankable paper will be given. 10 per cent discount for cash on note accounts. No property to be removed until settled for

* * *

My father found work on various ranches in eastern Colorado. I don't know how he met my mother, Bertha Williams, but they married in 1931. My oldest brother, Delmar, was born in Elbert County, Colorado in 1932.

The small family moved to Colorado Springs in 1933. My dad worked at a dairy in the Springs. He also worked for the Works Progress Administration building road and railroads for the government until shortly after I was born. He then went to work for McCarthy Plumbing, where he worked for thirty years until he retired.

I was born on March 10, 1935, in a house on West Colorado Avenue in Colorado Springs, Colorado. I'd like to tell you that it was a cold March day in the middle of a blizzard just to make a better story of it, but the truth is I don't remember. It could have been a gray winter day, or it could have been warm and sunny. That's the way Colorado weather is at that time of year.

I was the second son born to Delbert Humphrey and Bertha Williams Humphrey and was christened Gerald Martin Humphrey. I wasn't Gerald very long, though, as my older brother, Delmar, who was just learning to talk, couldn't say baby. But he could say babe. He called me Babe, and the name stuck. I'm still Babe to this day.

I ended up being one of six children. My brother Larry and my sister Carol were born next. After three boys, my mother finally got her daughter. Later on my brother Dean and sister Judy came along. My mother sort of raised three families. There were a few years between each pair of kids. I spent most of my play time with Delmar because Larry was a bit younger than I was.

Babe & Delmar with mother, Bertha

Babe & Delmar on horse

Our parents are gone now, but all of my siblings are still living. They are in good health and enjoying their own families.

We moved out to the country to Black Forest when I was four years old. My father had a friend named Earl Miller, who worked with him at the plumbing company, and they rode to work together, trading off driving each week. They drove twenty-five to thirty miles each way every day.

When they got tired of driving to town, they moved into the Springs. When they got tired of living in town, they moved back out to the Forest. Although the drive was roughly thirty miles then, it's only ten to fifteen today, depending on which road you take. Colorado Springs has grown to the north, east, and south. It would have grown to the west if not for Pikes Peak. Black Forest lies to the northeast of Colorado Springs at a higher elevation, perhaps 7,200 feet. It is a heavily wooded area in hilly country, and it is cooler in the summer and colder in the winter than it is downtown.

One of the times when we moved into town, when I was seven years old, we rented a house on a goat dairy farm. Now, we didn't raise goats, don't get me wrong. We just rented the house.

The former tenants left behind two sick goats. My brother and I nursed one of the nanny goats back to health. She became part of the family along with our old Guernsey cow. We lugged them with us whenever we moved, and as I got older, I milked the goat and the cow. I never did acquire a taste for goat's milk, although I drank plenty of it when I was young. The trouble with goat milk is that it tastes and smells like goat.

* * *

I wasn't a very good looking kid back then, and to make matters worse, I had to wear bib overalls, which did absolutely nothing for my image. I had long, stringy brown hair and an abundance of annoying freckles.

When I was eight or nine years old, a carnival came to town and set up half a mile from where we lived. I wandered to the carnival one day to look around. I got there just in time to see the featured act, Rover, the high diving dog. Someone had set up a tower that must have gone thirty feet into the air and placed a ladder next to it. Attached to the top of the ladder was a two-by-twelve inch plank. This plank stretched out over a big tank of water on the ground that was two or three feet deep. Some guy carried Rover up the ladder and put him on the plank, then pushed him to the end of it and into the water with a broom. Rover hit the water running, jumped out of the tank, and sprinted through the gate, never to be seen again. I'm sure the next show featured Bowser, the high diving dog, or some other mongrel that had the misfortune to be in the wrong place at the wrong time, but it sure wasn't going to be Rover.

After the show, I headed to the midway to look at all the rides. I was fascinated by the carnival rides then and still am today. I'm likely to climb on anything at least once if it looks like fun.

Just about the time I got to where the rides were, an unfamiliar lady came up to me and took me by the hand. "Now you come along with me, young man."

"Yes, ma'am," I blurted out, having no idea what was afoot.

She led me onto a stage. In those days, a person could do that to a kid, and no one thought much of it, not like things are today. Several other kids stood on the stage, all of them sprinkled with freckles, much like I was. The carnival sponsors were having a freckle contest, and the winner would be judged by the audience.

I got the most applause and was miraculously declared the winner. I probably won because I was the only one wearing bib overalls and the audience felt sorry for me.

The grand prize was a 200-pound steel teeter-totter. Now I had to go home and convince my folks that I had won a teeter-totter in a freckle contest. I was sure that the only thing that would happen was that I would get sent to bed without my supper for fibbing. I finally talked my parents into going with me to the carnival to see my teeter-totter. Dad had to borrow a truck from one of his friends to go back and get it and take it home. It had to be picked up that night as the carnival was moving on.

This didn't appear on the surface to be a big deal in my life, but in one way I think it was. It might have been the reason that I had enough self-confidence to enter other contests with my music. I entered several and was successful in all of them. After all, you can't win if you don't enter.

* * *

Life for me wasn't much different growing up than it was for any of my friends. We didn't have much, and cash was hard to come by, but we always had plenty to eat and a good roof over our heads. I remember coming home hungry from school, and there was always a loaf of homemade bread on the counter. I used to cut a thick slice, cover it with butter, and pour a heaping helping of sugar on it. Maybe that's the reason I'm so hyper today, all that sugar.

Some folks might think that we were poor, but we didn't give it much thought one way or the other. All of the families who lived near us were in the same boat. We lived the life of farm kids when we lived in Black Forest and town kids when we lived in Colorado Springs. We were happy and grew up with love in our hearts for family and friends.

We made our own fun, and I did what my older brother Delmar did most of the time. I tagged along with Delmar and his friends, and because I was the smallest, I was at their mercy. When we played cowboys and Indians, I had to be the Indian. When we played war, I was always the enemy. I died better than any kid in the Forest. I writhed in mock pain and grimaced with the best of them. I went on for several minutes before keeling over dead, draped over a log or fallen by a fox hole. For some reason, I put a whole lot more effort into dying when I was the war enemy than I did when I was an Indian.

Delmar used to get me into trouble, but he got me out of a few jams too. When we played rodeo, Delmar and his friends tied me on a calf and watched me ride. I never got hurt and rode a calf pretty good for a kid. They used to put me into a baby buggy or a wagon and push me down a hill just to see the wreck. It's a wonder I survived!

Delmar saved me one day when we went swimming in a cattle watering pond. I dove in head first and found myself in three feet of mud. My feet stuck straight up in the air. Delmar pulled me out of the mud and cleaned it from my nose and mouth. Then we continued our swim. We never dove into that pond again, I can tell you that.

When I was in the fifth grade and living in Colorado Springs, we rode the bus down to the South Side Boys Club. Delmar and his friends always lined me up to fight a Hispanic kid. I was a good fighter and usually won, but I faced the problem of getting out of there without having to fight the older brother of the kid I had just whipped. Besides a brother, the Hispanic kid usually had cousins. I always waited until the bus was outside and ready to leave before I ran down a long corridor. Delmar opened the door for me, and I hopped on the bus before those Hispanic kids knew what had happened. I did this often enough that I had it perfected.

During the time that we lived on the west side of Colorado Springs, I became interested in going to church. I don't know where this interest came from because my family didn't go to church much. I used to slip into the church by myself, go up into the balcony, and listen. From the first time that I did this, I knew that God was going to be an important part of my life. Sometimes my Grandpa Williams went to church with me when he found out that I was interested in going.

* * *

I started school in Black Forest in a one-room school house with Miss Edith Wolford as my teacher. I got to know Miss Wolford well during the next twelve years of my life. In fact, with the exception of the brief time when we lived at the goat dairy farm back in town, she taught me at some time during every year until I graduated from high school. I had other teachers during high school, but every year I had Miss Wolford for at least

Black Forest School

one class. I couldn't get away with anything when she was around.

Miss Wolford was a disciplinarian and wouldn't hesitate to box your ears if she thought you had it coming. I will say that I often thought her inclination was to err on the side of discipline and not leniency. However, I never got a punishment that I didn't deserve. Cheating, skipping school, fighting, or lying never escaped her attention. Thank God she cared enough to keep me on the straight and narrow. It would have been

Plaque on school

Babe revisits Black Forest School

BLACK FOREST LOG SCHOOL

The Friends of the Black Forest Log School preserve and maintain the school building. As docents, they present local history and raise awareness of early public-school education. The building is owned by the Black Forest Fire & Rescue Department.

HISTORICAL BACKGROUND

1922 The Black Forest School opened for grades one through eight.

1925 or 26 A foundation, cloak room and coal bin were added.

1936 Mrs. Edith Wolford came to teach.

1945 Black Forest School closed after consolidation with Falcon District.

1947 El Paso County converted the building to a home used by the employee, who maintained the county roads.

1981 The county road department vacated the property, and the future of the building was in limbo.

1992 The Black Forest Log School was placed on the National Register of Historic Places.

1996 The restoration began when the roof was placed with the aid of a grant from the Colorado Historical Fund.
The School Brought Us Together was published with grant support.

1997 The foundation was replaced with another grant and matching funds from members of the community.

1998-2000 Restoration of the interior was completed, and local residents donated items to furnish the 1930s schoolroom.

Black Forest Log School with Historic Background

easier for her to let some things slide, but that wasn't who she was.

In later years, when Falcon High School got a Principal, Mr. C.E. Martin, he dished out corporal punishment by sending us out to cut a willow with which to get switched. I wasn't the best behaved kid in school, and it seems like I cleared enough land of willows while I attended that school to put in a fair-sized corn field.

In those days I took my lickings and kept my mouth shut because complaining to my mom and dad about it only bought me a worse whaling at home. I got kicked off the school bus more than once and had a long hike home through the fields. Like the lickings, I deserved the long walks. They were good for me. They gave me time to think.

In spite of her hair trigger, Miss Wolford was an excellent teacher, and I owe her a lot. In the late fifties or early sixties, when a new high school was built in Falcon, she taught there. She taught for years in the county and now has an elementary school named in her honor in Black Forest.

I was always a pretty good fighter, and attending a one-room school meant that in my younger years, there were always older boys who took advantage of the fact that they were bigger than I was. Bullying wasn't controlled by the schools then as it is now. There was always a bigger kid around to eat my lunch or to harass me in any way he deemed appropriate at the time.

One day, I decided to stand up for myself. I rounded up two other boys about my size and told them that we couldn't fight the bullies alone, but if we ganged up on them we could handle them. We formed an alliance. Sure enough, the next time one of us got picked on, my group of friends and I all took off after the bigger kid and whooped him but good. The word soon got around, and my buddies and I were left alone after that. One of the big kids, Larry West, later became my brother-in-law when I married his sister, Martha.

* * *

The house in Black Forest was far away from everything. Two miles to the store, two miles to the school, two miles to any of my friends' houses, and all I had for transportation was shanks pony. In other words, I walked. Back then the roads were all gravel unless they were just plain dirt, so I got to be a fair walker.

My mother sometimes sent me to the store, and it took me so long to get there that I forgot what she had sent me for. This upset my mother to no end and embarrassed me to death. One time she sent me for toilet paper, and I yelled *toilet paper, toilet paper, toilet paper* all the way to the store.

Often when something was happening at the Community Center, two miles away, the event lasted into the night, and I ambled the two miles home in the dark. The Community Center and the school were right next to each other. For you young bucks who are reading this, I should tell you that the road to and from the Community Center and the school was up hill both ways. You may have guessed that I got some serious exercise in those days.

When I was in the tenth grade and living in the Forest, I came upon a stray Pinto horse as I traipsed through the grass on my way to somewhere. It seemed to just be wandering around, so I slung a rope around its neck and took it home. Fancy me. I now had transportation, and I rode that horse to the store or to my friends' houses, even into Colorado Springs, almost thirty miles away. I never had a saddle, so I rode bareback. I didn't even have a bridle or a bit. I just had a halter and a rope and rode the horse that way.

After a year or so, a feller stopped by our house. "Say there, son, that looks like my horse. Does it belong to you?"

"No, sir, it doesn't. I found him in the forest about a year ago."

Off he rode on the horse, neither one ever to be seen by me again.

Some time after that I found a mule in the same way and rode him all over the county using just a halter and a rope. I eventually let the mule go.

* * *

Some of the houses I lived in while growing up had wells and outdoor plumbing (two-holers to be exact). I remember doing my school work by the light of a kerosene lamp on occasion and chopping kindling for the wood burning stoves. We had our chores to do, such as milking and feeding the cow and the goat, feeding the chickens, and gathering the eggs. We fed the rabbits and performed the other tasks that came with country life. When I had chores to do, it meant that I got up early, frequently before daylight, so I would be finished in time to go to school.

When it came time to buy school clothes, my mother handed my brothers and sisters and me the Montgomery Ward catalog or the Sears, Roebuck and Co., catalog and told us to pick out the pants and shirts we liked. She then sent off the order, and after a time, our clothes arrived in the mail.

We didn't have much in the way of entertainment in those days. Television hadn't been invented yet, or if it had, we hadn't seen it. We did have a radio, and I always hurried home from school and listened to the daily fifteen minute serials that started at 4:00 p.m. and lasted until 6:00 p.m. I remember *Jack Armstrong, The All American Boy*. This show was sponsored by Wheaties, Breakfast of Champions. Ovaltine sponsored *Captain Midnight,* and I recall a program about a fighter pilot, Hop Harrigan, and his co-pilot, Tank Tinker. Who could forget *Terry and the Pirates* or *Superman?* There were some westerns, such as *Tennessee Jed, Red Ryder, Hop-A-Long Cassidy,* and *The Lone Ranger,* which came on at 6:00 p.m. and lasted thirty minutes, as did the other shows after that. We learned countless country songs from the Grand Ole Opry, which was broadcast on the radio and later on TV, and the late-night super power stations from Clint and Del Rio, Texas. These stations came on late at night and were clear-channel stations that reached across most of the country.

* * *

I played some of my very first songs on the guitar on a borrowed instrument. I didn't have my own guitar. Delmar and a few of his friends frequently got together and sang. Delmar played his steel guitar, Calvin Burrows played his Gretsch guitar, and Jerry Thiebough played a harmonica. I was a bit younger than they were, but I wanted to play too. They let me join them, and I played Calvin's mother's guitar, an open-hole guitar as I remember. I got a lot out of those sessions. Thanks to Mrs. Burrows for allowing me to use her guitar.

I usually spent weekends with family at one place or another. I had uncles, aunts, and cousins who got together for Sunday dinner. Someone killed a chicken or two, depending on who was coming, and we all had dinner together. After dinner we sat around and picked guitars and sang into the night. Members of my extended family played a variety of instruments, and we got a pretty good songfest going. We sang mostly western songs and some old gospel songs that were popular in the day.

It was from these folks that I am sure I got my musical abilities. As I said earlier, my Grandpa Williams played a mean fiddle, and my Uncle Bruce Williams played guitar. In fact, Uncle Bruce gave me one of my first guitars. Dad had a fine tenor voice and could harmonize with anyone. He could also dance quite a jig. I remember at social events folks called on him to dance his jig. He loved to sit and listen to us kids sing and play our instruments.

My mother taught me three chords, G, C, and D, on the guitar that my uncle Bruce had given me. I loved it when my mother played for me. The song she sang, and the first one I learned, was

Little Patch of Corn, Growing In The Green Grass.
Little patch of corn, growing in the green grass.
Little patch of corn, growing in the green grass.
Little patch of corn, growing in the green grass.
Little patch of corn for you and me.

I think my first electric guitar was a Fender Telecaster cut-away, as I used to call it. I can't remember how I got it or who paid for it, probably Mom and Dad. I knew those three chords and thought I was a real gas. Delmar had a liking for a steel guitar that he ordered from the Sears, Roebucks and Co., catalog, along with a small amplifier. Carol, my sister, sang country songs. She wasn't very old then, but she had a great voice. My brother Larry played the bass mostly. Whenever we got ready to go somewhere, Dad always reminded us to bring our guitars, which we were glad to do.

Babe's 1st guitar, A Fender Telecaster

Delmar, Carol & Larry Humphrey

41

I had a friend named Delmar Hurt, who had a Fender Telecaster cut-away guitar just like mine. We won a couple of talent contests in Colorado Springs performing together. These contests were held at the Old Peak Theater or the Chief Theater. Both were movie houses, but they had stages. Talent contests were popular in those days. We dressed alike and had matching guitars. I think I picked out a boogie-woogie tune, and Delmar played rhythm. We used only the three chords I knew. We probably looked better than we sounded, but we won a trophy and a few dollars and got our picture in the newspaper.

Later on, we played for Delmar's dad, Noble, in a dance band at the Community Center, where the farmers gathered for pie socials, at grange halls, at the high school, or wherever else there was a dance.

* * *

By the time I got to high school, Mom had gone to work in town at an assembly plant of some kind, so she and dad left early every morning to drive to town to go to work. They woke me up before they left so I could catch the bus for school. Often I went back to bed and fell asleep. A friend of mine, Willie Roe, always came by my house and got me up and on the bus. If it hadn't been for Willie, I never would have graduated from high school. He and I were the best of friends, and I owe him for getting me through school. Willie and I are still good friends, and we still get together often.

During those years, I earned my spending money by working for local farmers and ranchers doing tractor work, haying, working cattle, or doing other odd jobs. Another friend of mine, Glen Ullom, and I did chores for several of the dairy farmers in the area when they had to leave home for various reasons. We gained a reputation for being dependable, and folks trusted us with their livestock and with milking their cows.

* * *

Music wasn't all I played in high school. I really enjoyed sports of all kinds. At Falcon High School, the students were restricted to playing basketball and softball and running track, due to the size of our student body and limited athletic facilities. We didn't have a gym, so we played our school basketball games outside on dirt. We drew the lines with lime just as you would a softball field. It was a game that lent itself more to passing the ball than it did to dribbling because one never knew when the ball would hit a rock and bounce off to nowhere in particular. The dirt was never completely level, and the home team had more than a distinct home court advantage as it knew where the soft spots were.

People parked their cars all around the court and sat in them to view the games. There were four schools in our region, and we played each one twice. In the 1950-51 yearbook, scores for that year were listed as follows:

Falcon 12	Ramah 31
Falcon 24	Alta Vista 7
Falcon 6	Calhan 7
Falcon 16	Ramah 35
Falcon 49	Alta Vista 26
Falcon 19	Calhan 23

By looking at the scores you can tell which days the wind was blowing, can't you? We played our basketball games in the fall, when the bigger schools were still in football season, and had our tournament around the 10th of December in Colorado Springs at the YMCA. We won the county tournament my junior and senior years.

I played second base for the softball team too. We had a pretty good team due mainly to our pitcher, Bob

Gieck. He was good enough to be named to the Colorado Fast Pitch Hall of Fame.

Most of the boys in school participated in track, and I also did well at track. I got my training from running home several miles after getting kicked off the school bus for one thing or another.

While in high school, I noticed one particular cheerleader, Martha Elizabeth West. I was smitten with her, but I could count a number of problems. One, she was taller than I was. Two, she was a preacher's daughter, which intimidated me a little.

The main thing, however, was that I wasn't very good looking. To make matters worse, my older brother, Delmar, was exceptionally good looking. He had black hair and wore a leather jacket and engineer's boots. People had a hard time believing that we were brothers. My scraggly brown hair and profusion of freckles did nothing but accentuate my skinny body. My sister-in-law, Jean, still reminds me of the differences between my brother and me to this day. Of course, Delmar is not that much better looking than I am now.

As it turned out, all of the imagined obstacles disappeared after a time. I grew taller and got better looking. At least Martha thought I was cute, and her father, the Reverend Ed West, made a deep impression on me. I grew to love and respect the character of that man, not just because he was a preacher but because of the way he lived. He lived the way he preached.

Reverend West wasn't always tickled with when I got Martha home at night after we started dating. I played in the dance band at night sometimes and it was frequently early morning before the dance ended. In those days, a date usually consisted of going to a show and grabbing a burger and coke afterwards. We smooched on the way home, but that goes without saying. Martha and I went together all through high school.

Babe's 1st car, a 1947 Plymouth-Leaded

Martha and I celebrated our 50th wedding anniversary with a party at the rodeo grounds in Jackson Hole, Wyoming. The party was attended by all five of our children, some of my siblings, and many of our friends. Funny how fast the time has flown. It seems only yesterday that Martha and I were still in high school.

Babe and Martha at their 50th Anniversary party

Chapter Three

THE MARINE CORPS

I graduated from Falcon High School in the spring of 1953, wearing the same suit that my brother had worn two years before. The suit belonged to my dad, and it was the only suit we had between the three of us. My two younger brothers, Larry and Dean, might have graduated in it as well. I don't know.

That summer breezed by the same as past summers had. I dated Martha and played in a dance band. If we weren't out late at a dance, we were at the drive-in movie. In those days, we could both go to a show, have hamburgers, fries, and a shake, and put a little gas in the car for under five dollars.

I got a day job or two, but I knew that I wanted to get away and see the world. I had always liked the Marine Corps and had always thought that someday I would be a Marine. This thought persisted from the time I was a kid growing up during World War II until it actually happened.

In the years following World War II, people stood in line to join the service. There was a more fervent feeling of patriotism than there is today. The United States had just won a World War, one in which almost everyone in the country became involved, either by active duty or at home working in defense plants.

In elementary school, kids took loose change to school and bought savings stamps that they put in a book that when full could be exchanged for Savings Bonds, or War Bonds. Folks collected scrap iron to be recycled into war machinery and even saved tin foil and rolled it up into a ball to be used in the defense effort. They also gathered milk weed pods and put them in gunny sacks and sent them to school with the kids. The government used the dried fiber for flotation devices. City folks planted victory gardens. The government even quit making copper pennies and started making them out of lead.

We fought Germany and Japan for our very existence, and everyone pitched in to help. Everyday in the newspaper there were pictures of servicemen who had been killed in a far off town in France or an island in the Pacific that most of us had never heard of before the war.

* * *

The Korean War had just ended. At least the armistice had been signed on July 27, 1953, after three years of fighting. Japan had occupied Korea during World War II, and when the war ended, Korea was divided. The Soviet Union controlled the northern half, the Americans the southern half. The Korean War started when communist North Korea invaded South Korea and captured the capital city of Seoul.

The United Nations Security Council voted to assist South Korea, and the United States led the peacekeeping forces. Twenty other nations were involved helping the Americans. China and the Soviet Union aided North Korea. The Koreans, however, viewed the conflict as a civil war. With the signing of the armistice, the border was declared to be the 38th parallel and remains the border to this day. Even though the official war was over, U.S. troops remained in Korea to guard against insurgents filtering across the border into South Korea.

Anyway, as I previously related, patriotism ran high, and Donald Fulsos, Jim Iberg, Roger Maggert, Willie Roe, and I decided to enlist in the Marines. We represented the majority of the male population of the senior class of Falcon High School when we went into Colorado Springs and enlisted on September 13, 1953. Willie Roe was not accepted as he had cut off the end of his trigger finger on a band saw.

The next thing we knew, we were on a bus bound for the Marine Corps Recruit Depot in San Diego, California, where we underwent basic training. Our Drill instructors were Corporal Sebastian, Private First Class Gomez, and Private First Class Riley.

Sebastian hailed from the south and had somehow found out that I was a guitar picker. "Hey, Humphrey, I like country music. Why don't you have your guitar shipped to you here?"

"Yes, sir, Sir. Right away, Sir."

When the guitar arrived, the first thing I had to do was learn to play the Marines' Hymn on the guitar. After a full day of training, it helped to sit around in the evening and play and sing. Iberg and I had sung together back home, so we kind of led off, and others joined in. Sebastian liked to listen to us, and our music seemed to compensate somehow for the drudgeries of basic training.

The Marine Corps housed us in Quonset huts, and I still remember how hot those Quonset huts were. A few weeks ago, I had the opportunity to attend my grandson's graduation from boot camp in the same place where I had been in San Diego, and it was just the way I remembered it from fifty-five years earlier. I don't think anything had changed.

Basic training was like nothing any of us had ever been involved in before. The purpose of basic training was not only to get us in shape physically but also mentally. The Marine Corps wanted to tear down and throw away the person you were and re-make you into the person it wanted you to be. The object was to turn a boy into a Marine who would obey an order immediately when it was given, without any hesitation.

It seems that the officers who trained us also wanted to find out who could swim wearing their full backpack. Keep in mind that a Marine's backpack contained all of his gear, ammunition, survival kit, medical kit, blanket, sleeping bag, gas mask, helmet, and weapon, among other things. Some of the guys told the drill instructor up front that they couldn't swim, but the instructor didn't believe them, so every recruit had to prove whether he could swim. Turns out, a few of the guys really couldn't swim and after a while had to be dragged out of the pool and have the water pumped from their stomachs.

Someone in the Marine Corps at some time seemed to have determined by trial and error the exact amount of time it took to prove that a recruit couldn't swim and how long it took to fish him out of the water before he drowned. I credit the time I spent as a kid upside down in a mud hole as being instrumental in my getting through this phase of becoming a Marine. As I recall, we did not suffer any casualties.

But that's how it is in the Marines. The training that one gets as a recruit teaches all Marines to operate as one. You know where everyone is and what everyone is doing. If someone isn't where he's supposed to be, one Marine or another finds out why and corrects the situation.

The hardest part of boot camp for me was the regimentation. We were up at 5:00 every morning, which was a brand new thing for me, and I had to do it without Willie Roe. Corporal Sebastian did a more than adequate job of replacing Willie when it came to getting me up at 5:00 a.m. every day. We then hit the parade field, and our day was underway. I had been used to sort of planning my day and doing what I thought was important. In boot camp, I realized real quick that we recruits were going to do what the Marine Corps thought was important. Looking back on it, I can see the wisdom in how we were trained and how it turned a bunch of kids who had never seen each other before boot camp into a well-oiled fighting machine, one that moved with precision and strength.

While in boot camp, we were given aptitude tests and skill tests to determine where we would best fit into the big picture. When we finished boot camp, I found out that a Marine Corps decision-maker somewhere felt that I could best serve as a machine gun operator and was given an MOS #0331, a Military Occupational Service Number, machine guns. I was assigned to Fox Company, 2nd Battalion, 1st Marine Division and promoted to Private First Class. I got a furlough to go home for Christmas with orders to report upon my return to Camp Pendleton, California for further training.

It was wonderful to go home for Christmas, especially with basic training behind me and a stripe on my sleeve. I couldn't have been any prouder if I'd been Caesar entering Rome. I had gone away a boy and come home a Marine. I think that all the guys who were in boot camp at the time that I was felt the same way.

I spent time with Martha and the family, and before I knew it, I headed back to California, this time to Camp Pendleton.

The first thing I gathered about operating a machine gun was that one's life expectancy was about eighty seconds if one didn't fire and then get out of the way. My instructors seemed to harp on this, so I took them seriously and concentrated on the training they gave me. Specifically, I made it my business to fire and move quickly. It occurred to me that if the average was eighty seconds, I wanted to get out of the way in fifty seconds or less, not wanting to bring down the average.

A machine gun squad consists of two gunners, two assistant gunners, and ten ammo carriers. I started out as an ammo carrier and worked my way up until I was the main gunner and squad leader. When I was made squad leader, I got my second stripe and was promoted to Corporal.

Camp Pendleton was a terrible place. It should be in west Texas. My squad marched all over those dry hills as we were put through our paces. I found myself on a first name basis with at least three rattle snakes. I think I would have become acquainted with more rattle snakes had it not been for all the scorpions. The sand dunes were really tough to hike in, and they were always changing.

The one thing that made Camp Pendleton bearable was that Iberg was there with me. He had been designated as a rifle man, and he operated a Browning Automatic Rifle (BAR). We didn't train together, rather we got together in the evenings with our guitars, and that helped to pass the time.

With our training completed, the powers that be in the Marine Corps put us on a troop ship, and we sailed off into the sunset, headed for Korea. The trip took nearly thirty days, and what a trip it was. Each of us was assigned a hammock that swung from the ceiling in the bowels of the ship. Initially I had to figure out how not to puke. The first few days were terrible until I got my sea legs and sea stomach. My mother was afraid that I would have a weak stomach when I got on the high seas, but I put her fears to rest when I informed her in a letter that my stomach was as strong as most, and I could throw my dinner about as far as the next guy.

Speaking of dinner, the mess halls on the troop ships were stand up tables only, meaning you went through the mess line and got your food, then stood up to eat it on high tables. When there was a storm, the ship rolled. If that happened while we ate, guys were thrown down hill into each other, knocking plates and uneaten food to the floor and making a considerable mess. I soon discovered that I could pull myself up by grabbing the overhead pipes, and I let the others fall beneath me while the ship tossed in the churning sea.

I spent my time in training sessions and cleaning my machine gun. I broke that gun down, cleaned it, and put it back together every day. Someone could bring me my weapon today, and I could dismantle it and put it back together blindfolded. Some things a Marine just never forgets how to do.

Jim Iberg and I soon found several other musicians on the ship with whom we got together in the evenings. We played and sang while the other guys sat around and listened. Here again my music helped me through some difficult times, and I would like to think it helped others forget their troubles a bit also.

When the ship finally reached Korea, it docked at Inchon. I can't describe or forget the stench that hit me when I went ashore. The Koreans lived in huts or in any shelter they could find. The smell of the cooking fires and the food they cooked, along with the smells from the lack of sanitation, was overwhelming.

Thankfully, my unit, the 2nd Battalion, was sent directly north to the 38th parallel, where we patrolled the new border between North Korea and South Korea. Our job was to stop the North Koreans from infiltrating South Korea. We were told that we had two jobs to do. Number one, report sightings of the enemy. The second, delay the enemy in case of attack. Fortunately for us, the North Koreans didn't attack, not in force anyway. At night the North Koreans sent a few guys to the 38th parallel to spy on our forces or to steal what they could, but that was about it.

One of my jobs was to take five guys out on night patrol and drop them off along the line and then go back and pick them up at the end of our watch. As one sat there at night minding the terrain, he picked out landmarks, such as rocks or bushes. Sometimes by the end of a watch, a guy noticed that a bush wasn't in the same place as he remembered it being earlier. The Koreans had patience and only moved a few inches at a time in order to penetrate an area.

This reminded me of western stories I had read as a boy. The Comanche used to sneak up on army outposts in the early days of the West.

My guys and I used a two-word password system. Each night we decided on a password composed of two names. If we came into contact with someone, we said John or whatever name we were using that night, and the other word was a sir name, such as Jones or Smith. If the correct sir name didn't come back, we were ordered to shoot on sight. I always got an accurate response, so I never had to shoot anyone.

One night in an area that I guarded, I watched an old Korean man, who weighed about eighty pounds, sneak in with an A frame, a special kind of backpack, put a barrel of heating oil on it, pick it up, and carry it off. I was so surprised that he could lift the weight of the oil on the A frame that I just let him go. He was a civilian and probably needed the fuel to keep warm.

After Jim Iberg and I had been in Korea for three or four months, we sat around the mess hall one day.

Iberg and I had our guitars out, and several GIs listened to us play and sing. A general and his aide were in camp and stood there while we sang a couple of songs. They left. We saw them but didn't think much of it. Two days later, orders came transferring us to Battalion Headquarters with Temporary Test Duty status. We were to be part of the Far East Country Music Show and travel all over Korea entertaining the troops.

Battalion Headquarters was just outside of Seoul, and within the hour Iberg and I were in a helicopter heading south. We went to a large warehouse where the duffle bags containing our civilian clothes were stored. After hours of hunting, we finally located our stuff. We had both packed some western shirts and jeans, and these were our uniforms for the next eighteen months or so.

When we arrived at the Country Music Show contingent at Battalion Headquarters, we found that there were ten or twelve guys already there, all with a country music specialty. We were put up in our own tent, so we were together most of the time. Dusty Sisson played steel guitar. One guy, Jackie D. Parrish, sounded just like Ray Price, while Dutch Shauntzenbach sounded like Hank Snow. A guy from Georgia, Shorty

Vaughn, played the fiddle. Iberg and I performed a Homer and Jethro act. Another guy presented himself as Uncle Elwood, a country comic. Doc Hayes, a medic, was a superb guitar picker and played in the Chet Atkins style.

I learned a lot about guitar picking from Doc, especially how to play chop rhythm. This technique is used in a band when there is no drummer to keep the rhythm going.

Doc showed up at "The Bar-J Chuckwagon" a couple of years ago. He was in town and came out to have dinner and see the show. We recognized each other immediately and gave each other a big hug. He had no idea that I owned the establishment when he came in. We had a good chat and caught up on old times. He ended up playing bass in a symphony orchestra back in Nashville, Tennessee, so music has been an important part of his life. I've never heard from any of the other guys since I left the Marine Corps. It sure would be nice to see them again.

Playing with this group provided valuable experience for me. Nothing I could have done would have been any more beneficial to my future life than this assignment was. No course I could have taken at

A SMALL but happy audience greeted "The Stringdusters," a 1st Marine Division Soldier Show, when it visited one of the more isolated Signal Teams in Korea. Traveling in helicopters from the 13th Helicopter Company, the seven-Marine cast traveled to the top of a 4,000 foot peak and performed in the shadows of the demilitarized zone. The show was the first to visit this isolated site. (From left) Comedian PFC William L. Barton and MC PFC Babe M. Humphrey.

Top Right - LR - Bill Barton, Doc Hayes, Shorty Vaughn, Babe, Tom
Bottom Right - Back - Babe, Shorty Vaughn, Doc Hayes, Bill Barton
Front - Tom, Dusty Sisson

Top - Jim Iberg & Babe on mike doing Homer & Jethro. David Fisher
as Cousin Elwood on floor with bass

Bottom - Entertaining the troops

any university could have prepared me so well. This was on-the-job training at its best. The only thing we had to do all day was practice and entertain. If we weren't doing a show, we traveled to one or jammed wherever we were. Come to think of it, we usually played as we went from show to show. All of these guys were good musicians, and we each took something from the others through the months.

We sometimes performed three or four shows a day, depending on the area we were in. We usually tried to do a two-hour show, and the troops ate it up. Sometimes a stage was available for us to use, and sometimes we used the bed of a truck. We made do with what was there. The audience usually sat on the ground wherever we performed. The Marine Corps did the best it could to get us sound equipment, but it sure wasn't like any of the equipment found stateside.

Before the Marines started supplying me, guitar strings were hard to come by, so I used communication wire. I found that I could tune it, but it was a note or two lower than regular guitar strings. Often when my mail came, instead of homemade candy and cookies, as the other guys got, I got a guitar pick and an A string. It was very much appreciated and put to good use.

The time spent with this group of musicians was where I really learned my music. We practiced three-part and four-part harmony, and we used it in the shows. Along with the harmony, we worked on our guitar playing, our timing, and our stage presence. Much of this has to come naturally, and I guess it did for me. I never could read music and still can't to this day. Fortunately, I can hear harmony and have the gift to be able to join a duet or a trio and add a third or fourth-part harmony. This has to be a gift. I don't know how you could learn it if you can't hear it.

To those of you reading this who aren't musicians, it may be hard for you to understand how we could sit around jamming half the night after doing two or three two-hour shows. All I can say is that you never get enough, especially when you're young.

After a while, the others asked me to be the emcee for the group. The Marine Corps had some special uniforms made for us, and I got a black and white emcee suit. I guess the Corps felt that it sort of set us apart having these special uniforms, but we attracted attention without them when we wore our western shirts, hats, Levis, and boots. After I was asked to be the emcee, I was on the stage all the time either telling jokes or being a straight man for Uncle Elwood, and introducing the other entertainers. Every one in the show played an instrument, so we all backed each others act.

We toured all over Korea either by helicopter, jeep, or truck. We got to see the entire country of South Korea. We probably spent more time in the back of a truck than anywhere else. It was darn cold in the winter and hot and dusty in the summer. That Korean dirt could be mud one minute and an hour later a real fine dust that got into everything. We had to clean our instruments as often as we did our rifles.

I attribute the gravely voice I have to that Korean dust. I ate a lot of it. Often, we stopped the truck to take a dip in a rice paddy pond to cool off and shed the dust. I always remembered the mud and the cattle pond from when I was a kid in Colorado and never dove in head first.

One time the group of us went to entertain at a high mountain observation camp. We had to circle in a helicopter for a long time to gain the elevation needed to get to the top of the mountain and land. When we were ready to leave after the show, the pilot couldn't get the chopper off the ground because the air was too thin.

I asked him, "What now?"

I couldn't believe his answer.

He declared in a calm voice, "We'll just taxi off the edge of the mountain and free fall until we hit some heavier air that will support the props. I hope it works out."

I hope? I suspect that that was not his first rodeo, but it sure as hell was mine. It was definitely white knuckle time for me. Obviously the worst did not happen, or I wouldn't be writing this book. That sure was one of those things that you don't easily forget.

The Marine Corps scheduled our shows, so we were out for several days, then back to Battalion Headquarters for a few days, then out again. One time we landed on the USS Enterprise to do some shows. I remember the ship's Commander's name. Humphrey. We visited hospitals, and we visited the Armed Services Graves Registration Office, where details of deceased service personnel were catalogued. During these excursions, we were treated like VIPs to some extent and often got tours of the facility if there was something to see. The Grave Registration Office, however, didn't rate real high on my list of places to visit.

* * *

Eventually all good things come to an end. One day our superiors announced that the 1st marine Division would soon be going home. The act broke up, and all of the guys that I had been singing with went back to their own units. Jim Iberg and I found ourselves back on night patrol duty as before.

One good thing happened after we returned to our unit. Jim and I were introduced to Jerry Morgan, who had arrived after we left. He was an amazing guitar player and singer, and we soon formed a trio that lasted for a good while.

A bad thing also happened one night while I was on patrol. I severely sprained my ankle. After hobbling around on it for a couple of weeks, I finally went to sick bay, where the medical officer put a cast on it, and I was confined to camp. I had accumulated a lot of beer chips by way of winning poker games or basketball games, so I used them to hire some of the guys to push me around in a wheel barrow while my foot was in a cast. There were plenty of takers, Iberg being one of them, and I took advantage of the situation. A beer chit was like a ticket a guy could buy to trade for beer when the beer truck came around.

Soon after we got back to our unit, Iberg and I had a chance to go for some rest and relaxation in Japan.

Our Commanding Officer didn't feel that we should be allowed to go. "You guys have been resting and relaxing, tooling around all over Korea for the last eighteen months as it is. You don't need any more R&R."

We argued that we were only doing what the Marine Corps had ordered us to do and were entitled to rest and relaxation as much as the next guy. Our CO finally agreed, and we got our week in Japan. When we got back, all of the guys lined up for a penicillin pill. Though I didn't need one, I got in line with the rest of the guys. No 20-year-old, self-respecting Marine wants his buddies to think that he doesn't need a penicillin pill after a week of rest and relaxation in Japan.

The next thing we knew, the First Marine Division was on a troop ship heading back to the states. Iberg, Morgan, and I entertained all the way home when we weren't eating, sleeping, or throwing up. After a few days, we did okay on the barfing part and looked forward to getting back on U.S. soil once again, even if it was at Camp Pendleton.

Eighth United States Army

Special Services

Certificate of Achievement

This Headquarters

takes pleasure in congratulating

PFC GERALD M HUMPHREY 14144434

in recognition of outstanding performance during

the appearances of the "String Dusters" *held at* installations throughout the Eighth US Army

Gerald M Page

Lieutenant Colonel, Infantry
Special Services Officer
Eighth United States Army

24 September 1954
_____
Date

Good old Camp Pendleton and more maneuvers. I was sort of anxious to see those three rattle snakes I had befriended before I went to Korea. I looked around in the area where they had been, but they were gone. I guess the scorpions got them.

The Corps was big on war games, and one day my squad was ordered to take a mountain, as it was known. My machine gun squad was in the advance company, and a helicopter let us out on top of the hill. I got my squad out of the helicopter, and we quickly set up our guns and secured the area. We waited for most of the day as the rest of my battalion was supposed to fly and land in the area that I had secured, but the weather changed, the choppers could not fly, so they all had to hike up the mountain to our location. We were finally relieved, and I tramped back down the hill to return to camp.

As I did so, one of the officers in command of the games hollered at me, "Nice going, Sergeant."

Apparently, one of the referees of the war games had radioed ahead that my squad had secured the hill in short order. I guess he liked the way we secured the area, and I got promoted to Sergeant.

Babe and Martha's Wedding

La Foret Chapel

In December of 1955, I got a new Commanding Officer. I went home on leave for Christmas, and Martha was home on Christmas break from Western State College in Gunnison, Colorado. Martha and I got married on Christmas Day in the chapel at the La Foret Retreat in Black Forest, Colorado. Martha's father, the Reverend Ed West, who was the minister at the La Foret chapel, married us.

Incidentally, Jerry Morgan went home to Arkansas at the same time, and he too got married.

Martha and I honeymooned our way back to Camp Pendleton. We rented a studio apartment in Laguna Beach, about thirty miles north of Camp Pendleton, and set up housekeeping. Later on, we rented a house with Jerry and Shirley Morgan on Cyprus Drive in Laguna Beach.

Married couples could live off base, and many did. We car pooled to work, which helped with the gas, which was up to thirty cents a gallon by then.

Martha got a job as a maid in a motel to help out with the finances. I continued training in the hills of Camp Pendleton. One day I got into some poison ivy and got it all over my uniform. I unintentionally brought it

Division Hillbilly Group Telecast Over Channel 10

The musical styling of Eddie Arnold and the comedy of Homer and Jethro went across the video waves April 7 in the form of four talented men of the 2ndBn1stMar. Their Country-Western singing was done in conjunction with the U.S.O month celebrations held on Channel 10, KFSD-TV, San Diego.

The group, composed of Pfc. Jimmy Iberg, H&SCo, and Cpls. Jerry Morgan, Gerald Humphrey and Sgt. Ernie Dawson, all of "F"Co, appeared on the "USO Canteen" show and sang two numbers, one in typical hillbilly styling and one rendition of the Homer and Jethro parodies.

The "Stringdusters" also appeared at the American Legion Hall in Vista on April 18 to call and play for the community's weekly square dance.

Winners of the 1st Marines' talent contest, the "Stringdusters," formerly the "Stringbusters," have a long history as a musical group.

Well known along the Imjin River in Korea for their western songs, the combo entertained their buddies on the lines and were part of the 1stMarDiv's Hillbilly Band that toured the Eighth Army area. They also were heard by the British Commonwealth troops in Korea on Radio "Maple Leaf."

Humphrey and Iberg have been "strummin' an' singin'" together since they were citizens of Colorado Springs, Colo., using their guitars and twangy voices to entertain "the folks" on local television and radio.

Morgan, a native of Warren, Ark., met the two singers in Korea and the duet grew to a trio. Dawson joined the group just a little more than a month ago.

75

home to Martha. She got a healthy dose of poison ivy and was sick for a while.

During this time, Jim Iberg, Jerry Morgan, and I continued to play music. On weekends when we had liberty we went up to Compton, California to The Compton Town Hall Party. This show featured the country western stars of the time. I don't remember that we ever played there, but we sure got acquainted with some of the performers. I remember Merle Travis, Joe Maphis, Rosalie Allen, The Collins Kids, Freddie Hart, who wrote Easy Lovin', and others.

I met Bud and Geri Isaacs, a husband and wife team who were talented entertainers, in Compton. Bud invented the pedal steel guitar. Geri was a yodeler and singer. We have stayed close through the years, and they filled in for us at "The Bar-J Chuckwagon" when we had a chance to sing with Roy Rogers in 1992. They live in Yuma, Arizona, where they entertained for years. Recording artists Speedy West and Jimmy Bryant also entertained at these town hall parties.

I had an aunt and uncle, Jean and Dale Devors, who lived in Redondo Beach, who put Jim, Jerry, and me up on weekends when we had leave, along with other Marine Corps friends that we took with us.

Jean and Dale fed all of us, and I owe them so much, especially for the food they put out.

Jerry Morgan, Jim Iberg, and I decided that we wanted to try out for the All-Navy Talent Show contest. We entered pre-qualifying contests all over the area. It was during this time that Ernie Dawson, who sounded like Eddie Arnold, joined our group. We sang a medley of songs that showed off our three-part harmony. Ernie played guitar while we sang. Then he performed a solo number, and we played for him.

We advanced until we finally qualified for the finals in San Diego. On a Saturday in San Diego at the end of August in 1956, we found out that one hundred fifty acts from Naval and Marine bases all over the United States had qualified for the finals. There were jugglers, tap dancers, magicians, and opera singers. You name it, they were there. The top five acts would get to showcase their talents on the Ed Sullivan Show on national television.

We waited all day long for our turn. It came in the early afternoon, as I remember, and then we waited for the results from the judges. We ended up in the top five and won a spot on the Ed Sullivan Show. Jim Iberg says that we came in third, but I've always thought we were fifth. I like Jim's third place better, so third it is. He was always a little smarter than me anyway.

I remember that one of the other finalists was a Navy guy, Jack Imel. He was a tap dancer and a marimba player who wound up on the Lawrence Welk show for a few years and later became a TV producer.

Anyway, we made the finals and were really excited. Those who coordinated the Talent Show told us that all of the arrangements would be made for us and that they would see us in New York City on September 20th for the shooting of the show. September 20th? Our enlistment was up on September 13th. The Marine Corps told us that we couldn't perform unless we re-upped for another three years. This was a chance of a lifetime, but was it worth another three years in the Corps?

This was one of those times when I needed some help from God to make a decision. Martha and I prayed long and hard and had numerous discussions about the right thing to do. I finally decided that it was time to bid farewell to the Marine Corps and go home to Colorado. Iberg and Morgan agreed, so we took our discharge papers over the protests and promises of the Marine Corps. Our superiors really wanted us to stay as we

Top Five Places All Navy Talent Show
LR - Jim Iberg, Babe Humphrey, Jerry Morgan, Ernie Dawson (Next 3 unknown),
Far Right - Jack Imel, - Later of the Lawrence Welk Show

were the only Marines in the top five. We were offered all kinds of incentives to stay, but we went home. I guess Ernie Dawson wasn't too happy with us, but hey, you can't please everybody all of the time.

I have never heard from Ernie since we left the Corps. I won't say that I haven't wondered what would have happened had we stayed in and had gone to the contest. I don't think about the outcome of the contest as much as I do about how my life would have been different with another three years in the Corps. To tell the truth, I can't see any way that it could have turned out better than it has, and I've never once regretted my decision to go home.

It appears that it could have been disastrous if I had stayed in the Marines. I had only been home for a couple of months when I heard that a jet fighter had crashed during training maneuvers at Camp Pendleton. It crashed into Fox Company killing several Marines and injuring many more. I could have been one of them.

Chapter Four

CIVILIAN AGAIN

On September 13, 1956, I got my discharge papers and headed home. We loaded everything we had in my green '55 Chevy, everything except the ironing board. We shipped that home, not smart enough to realize that the shipping cost was twice what the ironing board was worth. We've had a few good laughs about that over the years, so maybe we got my money's worth anyway.

Martha and I moved in with my folks until we could find a place of our own, and the first thing I did was get a job at Coca Cola delivering soda pop around Colorado Springs. The next thing I did was to organize a band. I called the band The String Dusters. The band members were Billy Reel on steel guitar, Deacon Jones, a short fiddle player (the fiddle wasn't short, Deacon was), and Don Wilmot, a singer and bass player. We soon lined up a bunch of gigs, and the band was off and running. The job at Coca Cola didn't pan out as well. I soon quit and went to work for Aircraft Mechanics.

The Aircraft Mechanics plant in Colorado Springs made seats for airplanes with a separate division that made automotive wrenches. I worked in the wrench division running a drop forge air machine. I put twelve-foot rods in a furnace to get the steel to a molten state, and then I stepped on a pedal and stamped out a wrench. It took good rhythm to work this machine efficiently. Since I got paid a salary plus an incentive for every wrench I could stamp out beyond my quota, I made pretty good money and rather enjoyed the job. In fact, I did well enough at this job that Martha and I rented our first house on West Bijou Street in the Springs. I owe Cy Scarborough, who worked at the plant operating the same kind of machine as I did, for getting me the job.

My brother Delmar and I had played in Cy's band before I entered the Marine Corps. He called his band The Rocky Mountain Rythmairs, and I still have an old poster he had made up that advertised The Rocky

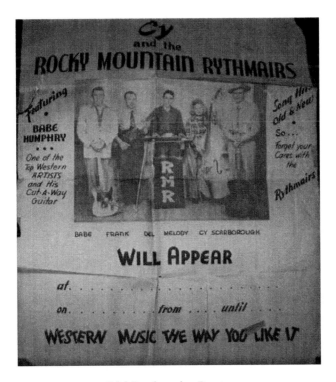

Old Rythmairs Poster

Mountain Rythmairs, featuring Babe Humphrey and his cut-away guitar.

Things were going smoothly, and Martha and I prospered. One day in early 1957, Cy talked Don Wilmot, Roy Friend, Chuck Camp, and me into auditioning with him to be entertainers at the Chuckwagon suppers at the Flying W Ranch. Roy played the mandolin, and Chuck played the guitar.

Don sang and played his bass. We got the job and played at the Flying W Chuckwagon every night from

Flying W Wranglers Circa 1957
LR- Chuck Camp, Babe Humphrey, Don Wilmot, Cy & Charlotte Scarborough

the first of June until Labor Day. We became known as the Flying W Wranglers. Cy's wife, Charlotte, also sang with the group.

The Flying W Chuckwagon had opened in the early fifties and gained in popularity every year. By 1957, work needed to be done to accommodate the crowds of twelve hundred people that the Chuckwagon drew every night during the summer.

Don Wilson owned the Flying W Ranch, a working cattle ranch, and had split it up between his two daughters after they each got married. A road ran smack through the middle of the ranch that divided the two parcels of land. Marian Wilson married Russ Wolfe, who opened the Flying W Chuckwagon on one side of the road. Etta Wilson married Gene Reid. They started a nightly rodeo during the summer months. The sisters worked it out so that folks could go to the rodeo first and then walk over to the Chuckwagon to be fed and entertained.

Meanwhile, Martha and I bought our first home at 525 Winnipeg Drive, a three-bedroom brick house, which we needed anticipating the birth of our first child. Sure enough, on November 6, 1957, our daughter, Diane, arrived. Life was good.

Not long after Diane came along, the building I worked in at Aircraft Mechanics caught fire and burned down. I transferred to the main building and worked at a job in the supply room. I found this job boring, and I no longer made bonus money, so I left.

I found my next position at Emerson Electric, where I was trained by a guy named Red how to inspect motors. I got along with Red, and he taught me a lot. I had been there for about a year when the manager called me into his office and told me that Red was going to be fired and that I was going to be promoted to his job. Now I knew that Red had done nothing to warrant getting fired and that he was a good, hard-working employee who deserved much better. The idea that a company would treat a man in such a way made me mad, and I told the manager so just before I quit. Red kept his job and eventually retired from Emerson, so I felt good about that.

In desperate need of a job, my brother Delmar helped me find work at Railway Express, where I stayed for a year.

It was around this same time that Red Foley, who used to host The Grand Ole Opry in Nashville, Tennessee, came to town with a traveling talent show. The talent show was held at the Chief Theater in Colorado Springs. The theater is long gone now but was a grand theater in its time.

Three of the Flying W Wranglers, Don Wilmot, Cy Scarborough, and I, decided to try out. We worked up a silly tune with Cy as a funny bumpkin. We called ourselves The Three Flames. Don't ask me why. I think Cy came up with the name. In fact, as I think about it now, I think we lost because of the name of our group. We should have had a western name. I think we placed third, but with a western name we would have won it for sure.

* * *

On April 20, 1959, Delmar hunted me down at Railway Express. "Babe, it's time to go to the hospital. Martha has gone into labor."

Before I got to the hospital, our second daughter, Jo Anne, was born.

Soon after Jo Anne's arrival, a guy I knew named Luke Butler, who played stand-up steel guitar, called me from the radio station where he worked. Station 5000 watt KPIK Radio played all country music, sun-up to sun-down. Luke worked there on Sundays as a disc jockey and a janitor.

"Hey, Babe," Luke inquired, "do you want to come down and see the station while I'm here. It would be fun."

"You bet. I'll be right there."

I stood rapt as Luke put records on the turntable. We visited while the records played. One time he got up to do some janitor work and left me in the studio.

I could see that the record was almost finished and yelled at him, "Luke, this record is almost over. You need to come and change the record."

"Just go ahead and put another record on. You can introduce it yourself," he shouted back.

Afraid that I would mess it up, I grabbed a record, put it on, and introduced it. I chose an artist with whom I was familiar. Luke left me there for an hour playing disc jockey while he did, I didn't know what, around the studio, and I had quite a time and enjoyed every minute of it.

A week later, someone from the station called me and asked me to come in and see the owner of the station, a fellow named Pappy Dave Stone, and the station manager, Ralph Searcy. It seems that they had listened to me the Sunday before, and they offered me a job as a disk jockey with my own show. I decided that this would be far better than the Railway Express, so I left the Railway and gladly took the job.

I had a four-hour show, which left me time for calling on established advertisers and lining up new ones for the show. This began a whole new career for me, and I had a good time with it.

Some of the other DJs I worked with there were Jay Drennan, Al McKinley, Arlie Duff, who wrote *You All Come*, George James, George Salem, Kenny Randol, and Li'l Herbie Hoflecker.

In 1960, Ralph Searcy went to Amarillo, Texas to open a new radio station called KBUY, The Town and Country Station. The concept was to play half country western and half rock 'n roll music. Ralph wanted me to go with him to Amarillo. He hired a guy named Cherokee Dave and me to run the country half of the station.

Martha and I leased our house for a year, and Russ Wolfe moved us to Amarillo in his horse trailer. Our third daughter, Lee Ann, was born in Amarillo on Pearl Harbor Day, December 7, 1960.

Cherokee Dave and I engaged in constant war with the other side of the radio station. We played tricks on each other, hid each other's records, and other mischievous pranks.

George Jones came to Amarillo one day and stopped by the station to say hello. I had met him in Colorado Springs, and Willie Roe and I had jammed with him in his hotel room, then drove him to Fort Carson to do his show. This time he and I played in his room all night long, and he didn't even make the show where he was scheduled to appear that night. He had a reputation for not showing up back in those days and got the nick name No Show Jones.

Martha and I stayed in Amarillo for only six months. The job didn't pan out, and Ralph Searcy paid for us to return to Colorado Springs.

The move hadn't affected my job at the Flying W Chuckwagon since I had been gone during the off season. We rented a house on Parker Street, our house still being leased out, and I hit the pavement looking for a job.

I went to KSSS Radio, a 24-hour station in the penthouse of the Antlers Hotel in downtown Colorado Springs. I convinced the manager of the station to give me a four-hour slot, 8:00 p.m. to midnight, Monday through Friday, and called my show Ranch House In The Sky. This left me free to play dance music on weekends.

During this time, from 1961 to 1962, mine was the only country western show the station had. Everyone called it personality radio in those days. I got a salary, and I also got commission on all of the advertising I sold. I sold my own advertising during the day wherever I could. It wasn't long before I sold more advertising for that four-hour time slot than anyone from any of the daytime shows sold.

At the same time, I had my eye on an old barn sitting on some land on what had been known as the Turkey Creek Ranch. Fort Carson had purchased all of the land surrounding the barn, and since the barn was empty, I figured that it would be a super place to hold a barn dance. I approached the owners of the barn and told them what I wanted to do and convinced them to let me use it for next to nothing.

I reinforced the floor of the barn, cleaned it up, did some painting and patching, and opened for business with my dance band as The Saturday Night Barn Dance. I talked it up on my radio show, and I drew a good crowd. I knew there was a need for something like this because in those days folks enjoyed dancing, but many of them didn't like the night club atmosphere.

I didn't sell beer or liquor and wouldn't allow it inside the barn. I'm sure some people kept it in their cars and slipped out for a nip now and then, but it wasn't the same as having an open bar. We charged admission and sold some pie, ice cream, and coffee, but that was about it.

This adventure didn't last long. The Saturday Night Barn Dance was only open for a month or so during the winter. When it got to be summertime, I

Rainbow Ramblers Dance Band

LR - Deacon Jones, Babe Humphrey, Larry Humphrey, Don Wilmont, Bill Reel

String Busters Dance Band
LR - Deacon Jones, Unknown, Babe Humphrey, Larry Humphrey, Delmar Humphrey

closed it to go back to work at the Flying W Chuckwagon.

* * *

I had always wanted to play the fiddle. My Grandfather Williams had played the fiddle, and when he died, I inherited his fiddle. In the early sixties, this dream of mine came true. I had the opportunity to learn to play the fiddle when I found a music store run by Leland Knight. Though almost blind, Leland could play that fiddle! He took me under his wing with a couple of other pretty good fiddlers, Larry Morgan and Byford Gordon.

This was another trial for Martha because if there is anything worse than a person learning to yodel, it is a person learning to fiddle. Hellish noises come from both. The dog used to crawl under the bed whenever he saw me unlatch my fiddle case.

Leland was a good teacher, and I was a willing pupil. Lucky for Martha, Leland had me out of the squeaky stage in short order. He could play the triple shuffle, a bowing art that few fiddlers ever master. Leland taught me the triple shuffle, and I am indebted to him for his patience.

I had been practicing for a year when Leland told me about the Colorado State Fiddle Championship at the City Auditorium. He asked me to back him up on the guitar. When we got there, he talked me into entering the contest too.

"What?" My mouth dropped open. "You've only taught me four good hoe downs."

"You do a good job with those, so come on in." He offered his special brand of encouragement.

I thought about it and decided to go ahead and enter. I had nothing to lose by trying. I think there were eight or nine fiddlers, and lo and behold, I finished runner up to Leland. I think he was as surprised as I was and just as proud. After all, he was my teacher. By the next year, I had had more practice on those four hoe downs. I still only knew four fiddle tunes, but I won the contest. That year Leland was runner up to me. We both had a good laugh because I had won the Colorado State Fiddle Championship and only knew four tunes. It was a good thing the judges didn't know how thin my portfolio was, or they would never have allowed me to win.

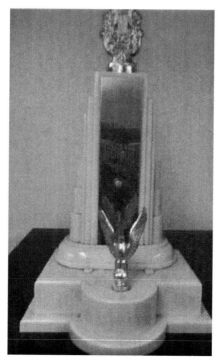

Colorado State Fiddle Champion Trophy

* * *

Colorado Springs was different back in those days than it is now. The Flying W Chuckwagon was way out of town, grassy ranch country with gravel roads running everywhere. Wire fences and gates stood at the side of every road, and the wild life consisted mostly of rabbits and rattle snakes.

As I said earlier, Gene Reid, Russ Wolfe's brother-in-law, started a rodeo a mile north and across the road from the Flying W Chuckwagon. It ran nightly in the summertime and began early enough that those who attended the rodeo could get over to the Flying W Chuckwagon in time for supper and the show. I was the announcer for the rodeo, and I had to get folks from the rodeo, across the road, get a tin dinner plate in their hands, and have them in the dinner line all before the dinner bell rang at the Chuckwagon. This entertainment made an enjoyable western evening for tourists and locals alike.

The tables at the Chuckwagon, which were outside, had kerosene lanterns on them, and we used gas pump-'em-up lights for stage lights. We hung them on a beam overhead so the audience could see our faces. We always lit a huge camp fire just before the show between the stage and our guests for atmosphere. I will never forget how much smoke and how many flying bugs we swallowed during the course of the season.

In 1961 Don Wilmot left, and the remaining members of the band hired Bob Minser to sing tenor. The band then included Cy Scarborough, Chuck Camp, Bob Minser, and me. In 1962, Buck Teeter, who sang and played bass, joined the group. The five of us were Introduced in the Western Music Hall of Fame on November 21, 2009

Back - Cy Scarborough, Bob Minser, Buck Teeter,
Front - Babe Humphrey, Chuck Camp

LR- Buck Teeter, Cy Scarborough, Bob Minser, Jack Smith, Babe Humphrey, Chuck Camp

Buck was a notable guy. He had been playing in a local band called Buddies of the West. He wrote songs and was a western artist. His paintings were in demand all over the country, and everything he painted sold before he finished it. Jack Smith, a shirt-tail relative of Russ Wolfe's, was with us for a summer or two at this time and sang *Old Shep* each night.

Three Indians from Taos, New Mexico dressed up in their native costumes and also performed with us, dancing several Indian dances. Their names were Mike Concha, who later became governor of the Taos Tribe in Taos, New Mexico, Joe David Marcas, and Sonny Montoya. Mike chanted while the others danced.

If you've never been to one of our Chuckwagon suppers, you need to know that the entertainers also help to serve the food as well as refill coffee and lemonade before the show. It's a cozy atmosphere, a good family show, and fun for us and for the audience.

Russ Wolfe introduced the Wranglers, and the show began. Halfway through the show, Russ popped up on stage to tell a cowboy joke. While he told the joke, the rest of us climbed a huge rocky hill behind the outdoor stage. We crawled to the top of the hill where the crowd could not see us and sang a song after Russ finished with his joke. This was an effective part of the show.

One evening, Russ told the joke, and we started climbing. About halfway up the hill, Cy tripped and fell. It seemed like it took three minutes for him to trip, slip, fall, and slide before he stopped. He moaned and grunted all the way. The entire audience heard the commotion but had no idea the cause of the ruckus. I was so tickled at hearing Cy fall behind me that I had a hard time going down to help him back up the hill.

We finally got to the top but were laughing so hard that we couldn't sing a note. Cy giggled and groaned for another five minutes. Our guests still didn't know what was going on and simply listened to the laughing in the dark. The song never got sung. Finally, we just rolled down the hill, appeared on the stage, and tried to explain what had just happened. For some reason, the audience never thought it was as funny as we did.

We also used to sing *Ghost Riders In The Sky* from that same hill while one of the ranch hands rode a white horse behind the crowd and up the walking trail behind where folks ate dinner. The horse sometimes got a little gassy and emitted the appropriate sounds with every jump. Most folks thought it was funny, but there were a few who found it gross, so we cut it out of the act.

On a warm, sunny afternoon, July 28, 1962, one of the future Bar J Wranglers was born. Martha gave birth to our fourth child and first boy, Delbert Scott Humphrey. Martha and I named him after my dad, his grandpa. I was tickled to death to finally have a son, as I am sure most guys would be. Don't get me wrong. Daughters are swell, but it's nice to have both girls and boys in a family. Boys sure are different to raise, however!

* * *

One night after the show ended and all the folks had gone home, Cy and I shot a bear. It had come down from the hills to rummage through the garbage cans. Back in those days, we handled situations like that ourselves instead of calling someone to tranquilize the animal and drag it away. Looking back, I'm not sure our way was the best way. We had a hard time finishing the bear off. We completed the task only after he had made a lumber pile out of a small shed.

On another occasion, as Cy and I drove from Colorado Springs to work at the Flying W Chuckwagon one morning, we spotted a nice buck by the side of the road during deer season. I rolled down the window, took aim, and dropped him right in his tracks. We knew better than to shoot from the road, not to mention from the car, so we hurriedly opened the back of Cy's station wagon and dragged the buck inside and headed for a more out-of-the-way place to clean him. I knew I'd hit him in the head, so I figured he was dead. Evidently I hit him on the antler and just knocked him out.

After a mile or so, the buck came back to life in the back of the station wagon, and I really had a fight on my hands. Cy wouldn't stop the car. He probably thought that he would have to help if he did. He bellowed at me to do something. I finally got into the back of the station wagon with my knife and slit the buck's throat but not before he had torn up the inside of the station wagon.

Looking back on the whole thing, I probably should have just shot him again. It wouldn't have made any worse of a mess and would have been much safer. After I cut his throat, the buck bled all over the back of the station wagon. Cleaning up blood and hair wasn't easy. All the guys in the band found out about it, and we took a ribbing for a long time.

One person who couldn't see the humor in the whole thing was Cy's wife. Somehow, I felt that she blamed me for the entire episode. I can see why Cy pointed the finger at me. In his shoes, I would have done the same thing to him. Cy's wife didn't like me much in the first place, and this incident didn't help matters at all.

If the truth be known, this debacle was probably mostly Cy's fault. My marine training had afforded me significant practice with a rifle, and I had earned the distinction of being a bona fide sharpshooter. Cy must not have completely stopped the car, or perhaps he let it roll just enough to spoil my shot, for I am confident that I would not have missed that shot unless something strange had happened.

While I'm on the subject of deer hunts, I went up to Meeker, Colorado on another occasion to hunt with Luke Butler of KPIK radio. In those days, there were a substantial number of deer in the Meeker area, and one could shoot two deer for each license one bought. In addition, a person could buy another license, making him eligible for four deer in all.

Luke and I left for Meeker right after the show at the Flying W Chuckwagon and drove all night. At one point, we traversed a gravel road that wound up a small mountain. We finally parked the car and went to sleep. It must have been 2:00 or 3:00 in the morning by the time we got there, so I stretched out on the back seat, and Luke did the same in the front seat.

When I woke up, it was barely daylight, and when I looked out the window there stood a nice four-point buck. I carefully rolled down the window, took dead rest on the sill, and squeezed off a shot. I missed the buck entirely.

Luke roared twice. The first time when he heard the shot, which must have been really loud to a guy sound asleep, and the second time when he hit his head on the steering wheel. He hit it hard. He had serrated dents in his head for a couple of days afterward. I felt bad about the whole thing. I think it's the only buck I ever missed.

* * *

In 1962, I wanted to try television. I strode into KKTV Channel 11 in Colorado Springs and asked about hosting my own show. Easy as pie! I did all of the work for the show. I was the emcee, and I found all of the sponsors. I interviewed mostly country western personalities when they came through town. The show was sort of like The Johnny Carson Show. We called the show The Western Hoe Down. I brought in some of the guys from the Flying W Chuckwagon and other local musicians to get them on TV, but the out-of-town names largely made the show popular. I had a studio band led by Buddy Watkins, who called his band Buddies Of The West. I always liked that name. My TV show ran for a couple of years, and I had a good and faithful audience.

While this TV show ran, I opened the Ute Pass Barn Dance in Green Mountain Falls, Colorado, which is up in the hills just west of Colorado Springs. KPIK radio sponsored it, and the format was virtually the same as it had been at the Saturday Night Barn Dance. People really enjoyed these barn dances, and I always drew a good crowd. It helped to be able to advertise on the radio and on my TV show. The family atmosphere gave young families and older folks a place to dance or just listen to music. Babies slept in baskets while their parents fancied the dancing.

Meanwhile, back at the Flying W Chuckwagon, the crowds steadily increased, and we were busy. Before the 1962 season started, Cy and I approached Russ Wolfe about expanding so we could buy into the business. We thought that maybe some kind of stock option could be worked out. Russ told us that he would try to come up with something, but he never did.

In the early sixties, I had become acquainted with a guy named Frank Vale. Frank owned a large furniture business, and I had done remote TV ads at his store. He had advertised with the radio and TV stations where I worked. He liked the Flying W Chuckwagon and often came to have dinner and see the show. He knew that I wanted to get out on my own, so he offered to put up the money to build a Chuckwagon in Estes Park, Colorado. I would be in charge of all the operations, and we would split the profits fifty/fifty. It sounded like a good idea to me.

Chapter Five

BEAUTIFUL ESTES PARK, COLORADO

In September, 1963, Frank and I went to Estes Park to see if we could find land that would be suitable for a Chuckwagon. We knew that Estes Park would be a good area because of all of the motels where the summer tourists who came to visit Rocky Mountain National Park stayed. We just had to determine the best location for a Chuckwagon. We finally decided on an old ranch named The 4T3, just a bit northeast of Estes Park. We made the deal and went to work on the new Lazy B Chuckwagon.

I had hired Bob Minser from the Flying W Chuckwagon to sing tenor and Paul Moyer, who had been working as a police officer in Colorado Springs, to

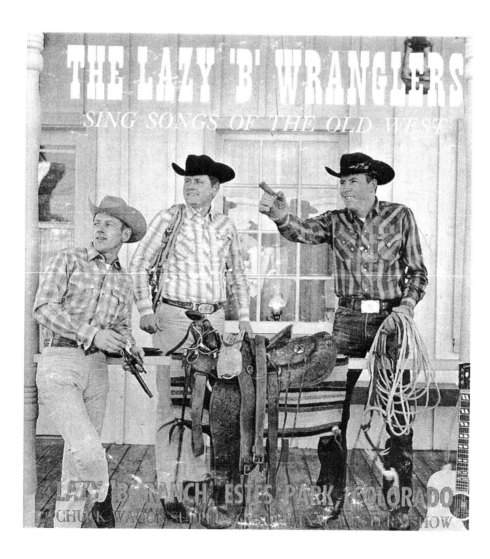

First Lazy B Wranglers on First Album Cover
LR - Paul Moyer, Bob Minser, Babe Humphrey

THE LAZY "B" RANCH IN BEAUTIFUL
ESTES PARK, COLORADO
PLAYGROUND OF THE ROCKY MOUNTAIN REGION

presenting . . . the legend of the western chuckwagon . . . .

In the Romantic old west, big cattle ranches extended from sunrise to sunset and a cowhand could swing aboard his pony at dawn and ride a straight course throughout a hard day without crossing a fence or leaving the land owned by the outfit for which he worked.

Many ranch owners sent out as many as six outfits consisting of perhaps ten cowhands and a Round-Up cook whose Chuck Wagon served as their point of departure each morning and their point of rendezvous each night.

It was the Chuck Wagon that carried the cowhands' bed rolls and personal belongings. Staked out at an easily identified water hole, it meant food, shelter for the night and a change of clothing. And the master of this point of meeting was that almost legendary character of the old west . . . the Round-Up cook.

It is the Round-Up cook who roused the cowhands with the aroma of steaming black coffee, bacon and sour dough biscuits hot in the Dutch oven by the glowing embers of his camp fire. During breakfast, the day's mounts were driven into a rope corral against the Chuck Wagon by the horse wrangler, or night-hawk. After breakfast, each man would rope his own mount, saddle it and gallop off for another Round-Up.

For the Round-Up cook, it meant cleaning up, loading up pots, pans and the cowhands' bedrolls, pulling up stakes and moving along to another big gather for the coming evening.

In the land of smaller ranches, where operations were on a more restricted scale, the ranchers would pool their operations with a single Chuck Wagon ruled by a lone Round-Up cook to preside at a point of mutual meeting.

For the smaller rancher as well as for the larger one, the Chuck Wagon became the meeting place for men interested in beef. This was the point at which they met to swap their stories and to trade their cattle. For them it was the initial center of community interest, the focal point of individual interests.

Our pledge has been and continues to be — to keep warm in your memory the best traditions of the Old West as exemplified by that almost-legendary character . . . The Round-Up Cook.

SIDE ONE
1. Bozeman Trail
2. Sweet Dreams
3. Tumbling Tumbleweeds
4. Lazy "B" Stomp
5. Montana Waltz
6. Place Where I Worship

SIDE 2
1. When Payday Rolls Around
2. Going Home to Montana
3. Twilight on the Trail
4. Boil Them Cabbage
5. Lord's Prayer
6. We'll Meet Again

we invite you to spend an enjoyable evening of . . . .

Authentic Chuckwagon Suppers and
Original Western Show *featuring the . . .*
LAZY "B" WRANGLERS

MAY THRU SEPTEMBER OR OFF SEASON CONVENTIONS WELCOMED • WE CAN SERVE UP TO 1,000 PERSONS

ABOUT THE WRANGLERS: In their short history as a group, the Lazy "B" Wranglers have won acclaim from the west coast to the Mississippi as one of this country's most standing "true western" singing groups. Their unique style of close harmony has captured audiences all-over through the medium of television, radio, and personal appearance. Accomplishments already include their own weekly television show originating in Colorado Springs, Colorado, and a fantastic reception at the famous "Grand Ole Opry" show, Nashville, Tennessee. We are certain you will agree after listening to this album that this group represents an invigorating breath of fresh air in the western field.

First Lazy B Wranglers on First Album Cover

sing lead. I sang baritone. Bob, Paul, and I formed a most unique natural trio because all of us could sing all of the parts. During our shows, we mixed and matched who sang each part to suit the songs.

Martha, the family, and I moved into a house on the ranch, and a couple of cabins there housed Bob and Paul and their families. I hired a carpenter to lead the construction crew, and the four of us went to work building the restaurant. When I wasn't working on the actual construction, I called on all of the motels in the area and visited Rotary Clubs and other service organizations promoting the Lazy B. We entertained all over the area, lining up customers for our first summer in Estes Park. As it turned out, I had done too good a job of this, and it came back to haunt me. I'll tell you about that later.

While Bob, Paul, and I performed in and around Estes Park before the start of the 1964 season, we met a guy named Gene Quaw, who was the music director for Montana State University in Bozeman, Montana. He invited us to come to Bozeman to entertain at the college there, and he also wanted us to look at some songs he had written for the upcoming Montana Centennial. He explained that he wanted us to make the songs western since his expertise was not of a western nature.

After the members of the Centennial Board at Montana State University heard our performance, they decided that they wanted us to take the songs to Nashville and record them on an album that they could use to promote the Centennial. We agreed to do this and drove to Nashville, arranging songs along the way. Gene had written some neat songs, such as *The Bozeman Trail, Montana Waltz, Going Home To Montana*, and *Montana Ditch*, to name a few.

A funny thing happened while we were in Bozeman. A guy who owned a club had gone to our show at the University. He asked us to entertain at the Belgrade Club, his bar at the racetrack in Belgrade, about ten miles west of Bozeman. We took him up on his offer to sing at the Belgrade Club. This was probably the wildest place I ever entertained. A whole lot of drinking went on, and to make matters worse, the bartender shot a rifle across the room at objects on the wall above where we sang, and stuff fell down on us as bullets went into the wall. I came a whole lot closer to getting shot in Belgrade, Montana than I ever did in Korea.

Album Recorded for Montana Centennial Circa 1964

When we arrived in Nashville, we went to CRA MART STUDIOS to record. We were joined there by Monty Montana Jr., who sang with us and helped promote the album. This studio was owned by Grady Martin and Floyd Cramer. Grady Martin played acoustic guitar for Marty Robbins when he recorded *El Paso* and other western ballads. Floyd Cramer was famous at that time for his piano rendition of *Last Date*. Grady and Floyd backed us up along with a harmonica player, Charlie McCoy.

The policy in Nashville at that time dictated that a group could only record three songs a day. I guess there was a reason for this, but it made our stay in Nashville longer than we had anticipated.

We put the time to good use and one day decided to see if we could get on the Grand Ole Opry. We went in to see Ott Devine, who was the head man for the Opry then, and told him that we wanted to be on the show. He explained in a nice way that the show was booked up six months in advance and that he couldn't put just anyone who wandered in from off the street on the Grand Ole Opry. We told him we understood and thanked him for his time and left his office. On the way out, I asked the receptionist what time Mr. Devine went to lunch. She told us at 11:30 sharp and that he came down the hall right past her desk and out into the parking lot.

We found a small, vacant room along his route, and when he marched past it on his way to lunch we sang and yodeled *When Payday Rolls Around.* Mr. Devine strolled on by.

Five minutes later, he stood in the doorway. "You guys will be on the George Morgan segment of the Grand Ole Opry show tonight. Be at the Ryman Auditorium at 6:30."

Before the show, we went to Tootsie's, a bar across the alley in back of the Ryman, where we signed our names on the wall, as was the custom. Tootsie's is where all the Opry performers hang out. A quick jaunt across the alley takes them to the back door of the theater.

We didn't have any of the flowery suits that Porter Wagner always wore, but we did have some nice, plain western suits that we wore on the show. We sang *When Payday Rolls Around* and a couple of other songs. We got to do several other shows in Nashville while we were there, including the Bobby Lord Show on TV.

Wranglers at The Opry
LR- Babe, Bob, Paul

Faron Young, a famous country western star in those days, looked us up and tried to convince us to stay in Nashville. I told him that the Nashville lifestyle wasn't the lifestyle I wanted. I knew enough to know that living in Nashville and touring around the country doing a show in a different place every night was not the life I wanted for my family and me.

I told Faron that I had figured out a way to have the audience come to me. I was told repeatedly that this idea would never work, but I have proved through the years since then that it can and does work. My family was more important to me than the fame of Nashville and the attraction of touring the country.

While in Nashville, we recorded an album for the Lazy B so we would have something to sell after the Chuckwagon opened. We used some of the songs on the Montana Centennial album on our album. They were good songs.

* * *

We continued to build, to entertain, and to promote the Lazy B, and when June 1, 1964 rolled around, we were ready to open the Lazy B Chuckwagon in Estes Park, Colorado.

I had decided that Indian dancers would be as good at the Lazy B as they had been at the Flying W.

So I got a hold of Mike Concha. "Mike, could you recommend some Indian boys from Taos to come and dance for me here at the Lazy B?"

"No problem, Mr. Hummeries." As usual, Mike mispronounced my name. "I get you some very good boys."

I trusted him, so early in the spring of 1964, Martha and I drove to Taos to pick up our Indian dancers. On the way home, between Loveland and Estes

Park, at 3:00 in the morning, we found ourselves in the middle of a horrible snowstorm. Three miles out of Estes, we could go no further. We got stuck in a snow drift and were stuck good.

I took one of the dancers with me and left the other two in the car with Martha. We trudged into town. The town was shut up tight, and we had a terrible time getting anyone to open their door. Everyone thought we were a couple of drunk Indians and wouldn't let us in.

Finally we found a pay phone, and I called Big John Gordon, a bachelor and mountain man who lived above town with his dog Coors. He was a big, gentle guy with a great voice who liked to recite poetry and tell stories. His appearance was anything but meek. I had used him for odd jobs and on the stage, so when I called him and told him what had happened, he picked us up and took us back down the canyon to get Martha and the other two Indians. We got there at the same time as the county road patrol, so the road opened, and we came on into town.

We also acquired an old German Shepherd we called Chip while we built the Lazy B Chuckwagon in Estes Park. He hated men and loved women, especially Martha. I couldn't even sit next to Martha on the couch without Chip showing his teeth and growling at me. When I came home late at night, which was often, I had to scream at Martha to call the dog so I could get into the house. He played around with us all day while we built the Chuckwagon and fetched chunks of two-by-fours that we threw for him. Once Martha came around, however, his full time job was to protect her.

One day, after he had been with us for nearly a year, Chip went up a canyon behind the house and tangled with a bobcat. That bobcat turned him inside out, and when he came dragging into the house, he could hardly walk. He bled from everywhere and had chunks of hair missing. We took him to the vet, and the vet worked on him and kept him for a week before we went back and got him. It was all he could do to limp out to the car. When we got home, he jumped out of the car, made a beeline for that canyon where the bobcat had been, and we never saw him again. We looked for him but found nary a trace. I guess he must have met up with that bobcat again.

Opening night at the Lazy B sold out. So did the second night. That's when the trouble started. In my contract with Frank Vale, we had agreed that all checks that were written had to have two signatures on them, mine and his. Upon seeing the immediate success of the enterprise, he told me that he wanted to change the agreement and add a third party to the signature list. The third party was his financial manager, and even though it still took two to sign a check, I didn't need to be one of them. This didn't surprise me because as the Chuckwagon had neared completion, Frank had made an allusion to wanting it all for himself.

I'm sure that Frank knew that I couldn't go along with this and would opt out immediately. Frank could get away with this because, up to this time, he had put all of the money into the operation. I did not yet have the stock that he had promised me. Frank owned the Lazy B, and I had no desire to stay there and contribute after he had double-crossed me.

This debacle ended our partnership as far as I was concerned, and within a week I had found another place to do my own show. A lady named Bonnie Meyers and her husband, George, owned a motel and were very supportive of us and sent a number of customers to us. Bonnie was also active in the arts, and we had gotten to know her well. In fact, about the time we had the problem at the Lazy B, she was directing the play *Oklahoma* at a community theater in Estes Park. Bob,

Paul, and I agreed to be in the show, and she re-wrote the play so we could sing some of our songs in it. I played the part of Curly, Bob and Paul had parts, and we got Big John to play Jud. He was perfect for that part.

Anyway, Bonnie had a piece of land by the Fall River that she said we could use. It was a flat piece of land on a pretty location, so we hurriedly built a stage and set up tables and were soon in business with the Fall River Chuckwagon.

We sent word around Estes Park about what had happened at the Lazy B, and most of the local motels and other businesses supported Bob, Paul, and me and sent the tourists to us. The problem was that we had done such a good job in promoting the Lazy B in the surrounding communities that we were fighting our own promotion and didn't get much business from out of town. Those folks ended up at the Lazy B.

Then the other shoe dropped. A contract that I had made with Bob and Paul came back to bite me. When I signed them up, I had them sign a contract with Frank and me that stated that if they left the Lazy B they couldn't sing at another Chuckwagon within one hundred miles for two years. Lawyers served papers, and suddenly we were in court. The judge ruled that Bob and Paul had contracted with the Lazy B and not with me, so they were bound by the contract. He also ruled that I hadn't signed the contract, so I was free to sing wherever I wanted to.

I'm sure that Frank figured that Bob and Paul wouldn't leave the Lazy B because of the contract they had signed, but they did. I hired two new guys to sing with me at the Fall River Chuckwagon, but this left Paul and Bob unemployed. It also left all of us without a place to live.

When the going gets tough, the tough get going, someone once said. I would be remiss, though, if I didn't acknowledge the hand of the Lord in all of this. Too many pieces fell into place to explain it in any other way.

A day or two after the three of us left the Lazy B, I got a phone call from a banker who lived in Loveland, Colorado. He asked me to come and visit with him.

He sat behind his desk and looked at me. "Listen, Babe, the bank owns a lodge in Estes Park that is just sitting vacant. I need someone to look after the property. You and your group can live there for free. There are sufficient accommodations for everyone."

"Thank you. We accept your offer." I sighed in gratitude.

That solved one of our problems.

Another place just out of town, Vogel's Lodge, too stood vacant, so we made a deal to rent it for the rest of the summer. We opened it up as a steakhouse. Bob and Paul would run the place and do the cooking so they would each have a job. This was okay as long as they didn't sing.

Within a week or two after the three of us left the Lazy B, we had another Chuckwagon going, a place to live for free, and a job for Bob and Paul. It goes without saying that it was a tough summer. Nobody got rich, but we did make wages and survived. We didn't make enough to take us through the winter, so when Labor Day rolled around, none of us had a job or an income.

* * *

While we were at the Fall River Chuckwagon, we built the Big Coffee Pot. We wanted something for people to talk about, so we built a gigantic, six-foot tall coffee pot. We constructed it out of sheet metal and put it on a pile of rocks so it looked like there was a fire under it. We had a fifty-gallon stainless steel coffee pot with a spigot on it that sat inside the shell and allowed

Big Coffee Pot

us to serve coffee from it. Folks stood around the Big Coffee Pot and had their pictures taken. It was a real conversation piece.

We schlepped it to parades and used it for all kinds of promotional events. We had rigged it so that we could put dry ice down the spout, and it looked like steam was coming out of it. We even took it to Arizona with us when we went there, which is the next part of the story.

STEREO

FALL RIVER COUNTRY

ESTES PARK COLORADO
BY THE FALL RIVER WRANGLERS

126

FALL RIVER
CHUCKWAGON SUPPERS
and Original Western Show

SIDE ONE

1. GHOST RIDERS IN THE SKY
2. TAKE ME BACK TO MY BOOTS & SADDLE
3. A COWBOY HAS TO SING
4. TODAYS SPECIAL
5. BAYOU BABY
6. TUMBLING TUMBLEWEEDS

SIDE TWO

1. TIMBER TRAIL
2. COLO TRAIL
3. PAY DAY
4. TWILIGHT ON THE TRAIL
5. CANNON BALL YOD
6. PLACE WHERE I WORSHIP

Babe Humphrey   Paul Moyers   Bob Minser

STORY BY RED FENWICK

Outside the Black Canyon Lodge at Estes Park, Colo., a slowly sifting snow blanketed the mountain terrain with deep ermine. It was the first day of 1965 and it was beautiful. The clamor and the racket of the previous night's celebration had gone with the new day. Now a deep and abiding peace settled over the log lodge where we had danced the night before.

A crackling fire in the huge stone hearthplace spread warmth and cheer over the barroom. On one wall from a wooden peg hung a pair of battered old chaps. A well used saddle hung from another peg.

Suddenly three voices merged in the harmony of The Place Where I Worship (is the wide open spaces). The voices were those of the Fall River Wranglers—three genuine western voices that blended in organ-like harmony. At that moment the scene was complete as any artist could paint it.

They were singing just for fun. They sing most of the time that way, because they enjoy it, because they love it.

That song session went on for three hours—three of the most enjoyable hours of music I've ever spent. These boys didn't know it at the time, but I review western-type recordings for The Denver Post. They weren't singing for my special benefit—just for themselves and a cluster of friends.

Frankly, friend, I don't know where you'll find more enjoyable western-type entertainment than that provided by these three dedicated boys—Babe Humphrey, Paul Moyers, Bob Minser.

Their lively-hood is ram-rodding the Fall River Chuckwagon Suppers in Estes Park, Colorado, where the "Ol' West" is preserved in a true Western atmosphere. This operation runs seven nights a week—June thru September. After an authentic chuckwagon supper, the Wranglers present a full hour show—family style. They sing of the things they love; the plains, the mountains, the stars, the dusty trails, and the blue horizon.

They're the type that sing with their eyes closed in deep concentration. When they sing with eyes wide open there's a smile on their faces, a smile of friendship and enjoyment in their work. Well, call it fun.

Personally, I don't know of any trio of this type anywhere that yodels three-part harmony. I don't know of three voices anywhere that more fortunately blend to give just that right color to the type music they sing—not hillbilly, not razzmatazz, not blatantly tear-jerking—just pure, rich, imaginative western music that's real.

And oddly, too, when you hear them you're listening to three real-life cowpokes. Each—Babe was born in Colorado, Paul spent most of his life in Colorado although he hails from Illinois, and Bob, an-Iowan-turned-westerner—has been a working ranch hand.

Now they're dedicated to the preservation of the Old and the Old West's richest music. When they're not working they're singing. And when they're not singing th composing their own songs.

Listen to Today's Special. It was born in a cafe when mused the sign in the window—Today's Special.

Today's Special—"One Broken Heart—I'd give away broken part . . ." Hear it, you'll love it. My predicti that this ballad eventually will become a part of Ame great western music. If it leaves you moody, set your m on Pay Day or Colorado Trail—and enjoy a western vac right at home. Here, music lovers, is a new experien western music. Take my word for it, these boys wil through to you and you, too, will become another f just like I did.

If you are ever out "Colorado Way," bring your family re-live yester-year with the Fall River Wranglers fo evening you will long remember.

Red Fenwic

Cantankerous Crit
The Denver Post

FALL RIVER ENTERPRISES ● 33⅓ R.P.M. LONG PLAYING DISC ● UNBREAKABLE UNDER NORMAL USE ● CLEAN REGULARLY WITH SOFT DRY CL
PLEASE DIRECT ALL CORRESPONDENCE TO FALL RIVER RANCH P.O. BOX 1636 ESTES PARK, COLORADO
FRONT COVER IN ROCKY MOUNTAIN NATIONAL PARK
PHOTOGRAPH BY MERLIN K. POTTS, CHIEF PARK NATURALIST

* * *

I had become acquainted with a gal named Dot, who owned the Pinnacle Peak Restaurant north of Scottsdale, Arizona. If you've never been there, this is the place where, if you wear a necktie into the restaurant, it is cut off with a pair of shears and hung from the ceiling. The specialty at the Pinnacle was a Mesquite grilled cowboy steak, a steak big enough to cover a whole plate.

A person needed another plate for his beans and bread and other trimmings. One could also order ribs or chicken if one so desired. Dot wanted us to come to Scottsdale and open up a Chuckwagon by her establishment. Bob, Paul, and I decided to go down and take a look. When we got into Phoenix, we decided to stay there for the winter and so set about looking for something to do to make some money.

I eventually determined that opening a Chuckwagon next to the Pinnacle Peak wouldn't work simply because I felt we would soon draw all the business from Dot's restaurant to the Chuckwagon, and I didn't want to do that to Dot.

* * *

As we ate lunch in the lounge section of a bowling alley in Phoenix one day, I had an idea.

I approached the owner of the bowling alley. "Hey, could we sing for you. We're pretty good."

"Go ahead," he rejoined without interest.

But when he heard us, he hired us on the spot to sing and perform a show in his lounge. The gig didn't pay much, but it was something, and as it turned out, it gave us the exposure we needed to get a better job.

Not long after we started at the bowling alley, a guy who owned Wild Bill's Supper Club and Lounge heard us sing and offered us a job entertaining at his place five days a week. We took that job in a New York minute. Bill told us that we had changed the clientele from beer drinkers to cocktail drinkers, and this put him in high spirits, as it were.

It was while we were singing at Wild Bill's that I met Waylon Jennings. He had been singing at another club in the Phoenix area and was leaving to go to Nashville. The club where we were and the club where he was were two of the most successful clubs in the area at that time that played country and western music. The clubs somewhat competed with each other, although our club catered to the middle-aged folks while his club still had the young people. Waylon wanted to know if we could use his steel guitar player and his drummer. He wanted to help them find jobs before he left. I told him that we had never had a drummer or a steel guitar player and that we didn't even use electric guitars. He couldn't believe that we could draw the crowds we did with two open-hole guitars, a bass, and one microphone.

While we sang at Wild Bills, we got a call from a guy who owned a Lincoln Dealership in Phoenix. He wanted to sponsor a TV show, featuring us, on KTVK Channel 3. He thought we could sell his Lincolns. We thought it sounded like a kick. The show aired on Saturdays and didn't interfere with our job at Wild Bill's. The name of the show was The Bunkhouse Show, and it went over really well.

Another interesting thing happened during this period. A guy named Marvin Grigsby, who had seen us on TV, owned a motel in the area. He was also the pilot for the Sons Of The Pioneers, a famous western singing group. We met with him, and to my surprise, he offered us the name, the Sons Of The Pioneers.

ARIZONA TELEVISION CO.

ABC TELEVISION

3435 NORTH 16th STREET • PHOENIX 16 • ARIZONA • AM 6•5691

March 8, 1966

Mr. Marvin Grigsby
General Manager
The Wranglers, Inc.
4224 North 12th Street
Phoenix, Arizona

Dear Mr. Grigsby:

Channel 3 management feels priviledged to feature
your "Wrangler" program on our station every Saturday
afternoon from 4:30-5:00 P.M.

Your program is without a doubt the finest locally
produced show Channel 3 has carried since going on
the air 10 years ago. Your style of western singing
has brought to this market a new rendition of the old
west in song.

The viewing response has been tremendous. We have received hundreds of letters and many calls.

We feel honored our station introduced you to this
market and look forward to a long association.

Sincerely,

James Perry
Sales Manager

JP:bc

Letter from KTVK TV Station

131

The original singing members of the Sons Of The Pioneers were Bob Nolan, Roy Rogers (Leonard Slye), and Tim Spencer. The Farr brothers were the back up musicians for the Sons. Hugh Farr played fiddle and sometimes sang with the group, and Carl Farr played the guitar. As Bob, Roy, and Tim left to pursue other interests, they were replaced by Tommy Doss, Lloyd Perryman, and Dale Warren.

The three singing members of the Sons and Hugh Farr had a huge fight. They fought over who owned the name. The whole mess landed in court, and a judge ruled that as long as the second trio stayed together as a trio they could keep the name, but if the trio split up, the name became the property of Hugh Farr, who was the senior member of the group.

Hugh hedged his bets and sold an option to buy the name to Marvin Grigsby. Now Marvin offered it to us. We didn't really want the name and didn't think it would do us much good, *but we* visited with Bob Nolan and Tim Spencer all the same. In the end, we decided not to take the name.

I did get to spend some quality time with Bob Nolan. I remember the guys and I went over to his place and sat out in his wood shed and talked shop one whole afternoon. The Sons Of The Pioneers were my idols growing up. This group had a huge influence on me and the type of music I wanted to sing. To be able to sit there and pick Bob's brain about song writing, harmonizing, and the business in general was a dream come true. Bob then took us over to Tim Spencer's place, and we visited some more. Tim and Bob had heard our trio and knew what we did and were very supportive and complimentary to us. This was a true learning experience for me, and I will always remember it.

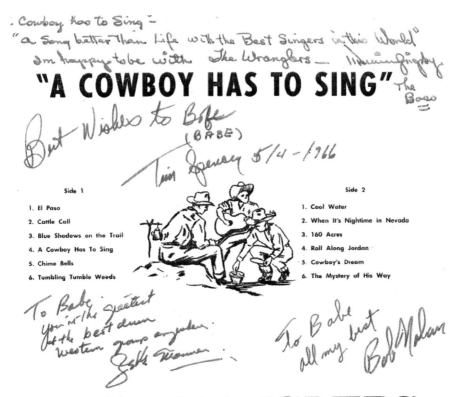

Album Cover with Two of the original Sons of Pioneers Autographs
Bob Nolan and Tim Spencer

We also listened to Marvin Grigsby. He told us about different promotions that the Sons had done. One idea in particular that the Sons had only discussed really fascinated us. They had talked about riding horseback across the country, entertaining as they went, in an effort to promote themselves and to raise money for a good cause. We decided to pursue this notion ourselves.

Chapter Six

A BIG IDEA

What a novel concept! Ride horseback across the United States, entertaining as we went. We talked about it and decided that it could be done if a whole lot of things fell into place. The timing had to work. Bob, Paul, and I all called our wives. All of us agreed that it made sense for us guys to stay in Phoenix and plan the ride while our wives stayed in Colorado to run the Fall River Chuckwagon in the summer just ahead with the entertainers I had already lined up. After all, Bob and Paul couldn't sing at the Fall River for another year, and we needed something to do in the summer.

Two things definitely had to happen for us to be able to pull this trip off. Number one, we needed a cause. Second, we needed some sponsors to pay for it. Marvin Grigsby called the Damon Runyon Cancer Research Foundation and told someone there of our concept. The person he spoke with liked our idea and said that he would present it to his board of directors. We sent him a record of our songs so he would have some idea of what we sounded like and to show him that we were a legitimate group who could do what we proposed. The board of directors of the Damon Runyon Cancer Research Foundation at that time included some real heavy weights in the entertainment business. Arthur Godfrey was the president, and John Daley and Milton Berle were also on the board.

Damon Runyon was sort of a local boy who made good. Though he was born in Kansas, he grew up in Pueblo, Colorado, just down the road from Colorado Springs. He followed his father and grandfather into the newspaper business, beginning in Pueblo and later working for several papers in the Denver area. In 1910 he moved to New York City where, for the next ten years, he covered the New York Giants and professional boxing for the *New York American* newspaper. He was also the Hearst newspaper's baseball columnist for years. He was inducted into the Baseball Hall of Fame in 1967 in the writers section and was also a member of Boxing's Hall of Fame. He was best known for his short stories celebrating the world of Broadway in New York City, which grew out of the Prohibition era. A couple of his stories were combined to create the Broadway hit musical *Guys and Dolls*.

Runyon, who spent the last years of his life voiceless because of cancer surgery, died of cancer on December 15, 1946, in New York City. In February of 1947, the Damon Runyon Cancer Research Foundation was incorporated in the State of New York in his honor. At the date of our trek, it had raised over twenty-six million dollars for cancer research. We were mighty proud to be associated with this organization.

The way we wanted to structure the trek was to have the Damon Runyon Foundation line up all the publicity. It would have all of the major press, such as the Associated Press and United Press International, follow us on the trek and announce our location on the news each day. Theoretically, the local news people along the way would announce to their listening audience the estimated time that we would arrive in their area. They would also advertise for our shows. We would obtain sponsors to take care of our expenses, and we would turn over all of the proceeds of our shows after expenses to the fund.

We all knew that it would be next to impossible for us to sell tickets along the way, so some of our shows would be free to the audience. We would have to depend on the generosity of the public and service organizations for donations for the fund. The only revenue we would realize was what we made from the sales of our records along the way. We hoped to get some publicity for the Fall River Chuckwagon too.

Now that we had decided on a cause, we had to go to work to get sponsors for our equipment and expenses. We decided that we needed a pickup and a trailer, four horses, so one could rest every fourth day, a motor home, an advance man who would be paid from the donations received, and a horse trainer to take care of the horses and keep them in good health.

We got out a map and plotted the course we wished to follow. We wanted to travel alongside the main highways as much as possible, figuring that in most cases we could keep our horses farther away from the traffic than if we were on secondary roads. We also thought that we would get more exposure on the major routes. We would ride along the new interstate system wherever we could, but it had not been completed in a lot of places.

We planned to leave Los Angeles on July 6, 1966. We had a commitment to be in New York City on November 4th for the big reception scheduled for our arrival by the Runyon people. We found that to follow the path we planned to take, we would have to average thirty-one miles a day, which was doable if we didn't get too far behind at the beginning while horses and riders got broken in. We knew we couldn't start out at thirty-one miles per day, but we also knew that later on we could do better than that to make up the average. Then we needed to get the equipment.

We decided that we wanted a Miley horse trailer big enough to haul four horses with a compartment in it that would serve as a dressing room so we could change clothes and get cleaned up for the evening shows.

I called the Miley Company. "This is Babe Humphrey. I have a singing group, and we're going to trek on horseback from Los Angeles to New York. We need a horse trailer..."

"Say no more, Mr. Humphrey. Miley will be happy to provide a trailer that will suit your needs."

"That went pretty good. Now let's see if we can get something to pull it with."

We all laughed at my small accomplishment.

All of us liked Chevrolet, so Marvin called a promotion person at Chevy and told him how much we liked Chevy trucks and asked if Chevy could help us out. Again, the answer came in the affirmative. He told us to go down to Rudolph Chevrolet in Phoenix, and Rudolph's would fix us up. Rudolph's painted our Fall River Wranglers logo on the door as well as other advertising, and we had a pick-up to pull the horse trailer.

Now we needed a car for our advance man to drive, so Ford motor company was contacted and the Ford representative sent us to Berge Ford in Mesa, Arizona. Berge gave us a Ford Mustang. Things were going so well that we decided to try to get a motor home too. Clark Equipment gave us the use of a Clark Cortez motor home.

We paid a visit to Porter Saddles in Phoenix, and this company had special, custom-fit saddles made for each of us. Tony Lama provided us each with three pairs of boots, all custom made and fit. Bailey Hat Company provided us with hats for the trek, and Gross

Suits of Denver gave us our show suits. Marvin told the Levi Strauss Company that we preferred Levis to Wranglers, and Levi outfitted us through Saba's, a western store in Scottsdale. Fender furnished new guitars for Paul and me. and Kay furnished a S-9 Swingmaster bass for Bob. Conoco gave us a credit card for all of our gas and oil needs, so that expense was covered.

The next thing we had to do was pick out our horses. We felt that they should be good strong mounts and should be three to seven years old. It occurred to us that we should contact the various equine associations and obtain sponsorships from them. I ended up with a horse that was half Arabian and half Quarter Horse. I named her Mare. Paul rode a buckskin Quarter Horse and Bob a gray Quarter Horse that he called Chaw. Our fourth mount, Big Red, was a fifteen-hand thoroughbred.

Now, I've said it before in this book and will no doubt say it again before we are finished. I have been guided and helped throughout my life to make the right decisions, and things have come together for me that I can only explain as divine intervention.

Putting this trek together was certainly one of them. We found sponsors for everything we needed to complete the feat, and what was even more incredible was that we were never turned down once. We made only one phone call to each sponsor. Every one of them agreed to help us on the spot and went overboard in doing it.

Chuck Kibler, a guy I knew and an outstanding horse trainer, really knew his business. He would drive the pickup that pulled the horse trailer. His wife Kitty wanted to go too, so she would drive the motor home and did the cooking.

Somehow Jayne Mansfield, the actress, got involved and was the Guiding Star for the trek. I argued that she would be of more value as the cook, but Martha voted for Kitty Kibler, and since Martha knew a whole lot more about cooking than I did, we took her advice. Lee Horn went along and handled the publicity and was our photographer. Blacky Austin, our advance man, traveled twenty or thirty miles ahead of us, lining up service groups, church groups, or anyone else who would host our evening shows.

* * *

With everything in place and with much encouragement and good wishes from dignitaries across the country, we were ready to go to New York. Thirty-one hundred miles on a horse in one hundred days. We must have been crazy!

The Great
TREK
on horseback

1966

IN COOPERATION WITH The Damon Runyon Memorial Fund for Cancer Research, Inc.

144

Chapter Seven

THE GREAT TREK

July 6, 1966, a perfect day in Southern California. We assembled in a park in Hollywood to start the Great Trek. We shook hands, slapped shoulders, and took pictures for the press. Jayne Mansfield attended the event as did other celebrities, who all looked for a chance to jump in front of the camera. The governor of California, Edmund G. Brown, and the governor of Arizona, Sam Goddard, both attended. We received a telegram from Arthur Godfrey, a popular radio personality and president of the Damon Runyon Cancer Research Foundation. He wished us God speed and a safe ride. I have to admit that the Damon Runyon people did it up right. It was a first-class party and a fitting send-off. We loaded the horses into the trailer and bade the multitudes farewell.

The trek was under way. We took the horses in the trailer out of the congested downtown area to the town of Duarte before we mounted up. This was done at the request of the local authorities, and we complied with the suggestion.

We had ridden the horses and let them get used to us, but folks honking and waving as they passed, along with all of the other distractions a ride like that was bound to have, took some getting used to. The first thing we ascertained was that when something came along to spook the horses, their first reaction was to jump toward the center of the road. I guess they felt that this was a safe maneuver to get away from a barking dog or a noisy horde of people. They didn't realize that they might be jumping into the path of a speeding car or a loaded semi.

We didn't make too much time that first day. We didn't come near the thirty-one miles a day we needed to ride for a couple of weeks, not until the horses and the riders were broken in. By the end of the third day, I wondered if we had made a big mistake with this undertaking. By the end of the fourth day, I was sure of it.

The guys and I were so stiff that we could barely get off of our horses after the day's ride. Thanks to all of our publicity however, and the shows we had booked, quitting wasn't an option, and none of us seriously considered it.

As the days progressed, the ride got easier, and fewer things frightened the horses. We had shows booked that we looked forward to, and as we got out into the country, the ride became more fascinating and less eventful.

We didn't always camp where we were going to perform. We made camp, got cleaned up, and then drove into town, sometimes ahead of where we were camped and sometimes back where we had already been. As I remember, our first show was on July 7th in Monrovia, California. By the 10th, we were in Barstow, California, where we performed at The Bun Boy and on radio station KWTC.

I need to tell you right now that one mistake I made was in not keeping a daily log of this trip. Maybe somebody did, but it wasn't me. I did save some newspaper clippings, but I have forgotten much in the last forty-two years about the details of the trek. It never occurred to me that I might want to write about it some day.

Anyway, I'm trying to piece it together from the clippings I saved and from what I can remember. Maybe it's a good thing I don't have all of the details as that might make a longer story than you would want to read. This way you will just get the highlights and the lowlights, which are probably the most interesting anyway.

On July 16th, we rode into Las Vegas, Nevada. A local riding club met us and rode the last ten miles into town with us. This happened regularly on the trek. This was a good thing because it made the local population more aware of who we were and what we were doing, thus getting a higher attendance at our evening shows. On the Saturday and Sunday that we spent in Las Vegas, we performed at the Appaloosa Horse Show and at the Stardust and Dunes hotels.

By this time, the going had gotten easier. The saddle sores turned into calluses, and with the wide open spaces of Nevada, we made better time. We found that if we walked the horses for ten minutes, trotted for five, and loped for ten to twelve minutes, we could make pretty good time.

We were really fortunate to have Chuck Kibler with us to look after the horses. He took real good care of them and checked on them to make sure that nothing ailed them. Being a professional horse trainer, Chuck knew his stuff. He was also a farrier and changed the horses' shoes on their day off when they needed it.

One thing I might suggest to any of you who are considering riding horseback across Southern California and Southern Nevada. Don't do it in July! Whew! That was one hot ride.

When we left Las Vegas and headed up toward St. George, Utah, the freeway wasn't finished through the Virgin River Gorge, so we followed the old highway up Utah Hill into St. George. This was a real narrow road with not much room on the shoulders and even less when the semi trucks sped past.

We got into St. George on the 21st and did a show on the patio of the VFW Post. The newspaper clipping affirms:

To All My Friends & Fans Throughout The United States:

On Wednesday, July 6th, The Fall River Wranglers, (Bob, Paul & Babe) left Los Angeles on horseback. Their destination is New York City.

You will probably wonder why I would endorse a horseback ride across the United States. It all sounds like one big publicity stunt, doesn't it? Well — IT IS!

I'm sure you all know of the great efforts made by the Damon Runyon Memorial Cancer Fund — it is a continued fight against a most dread disease. The Fall River Wranglers plan to ride about 30 miles a day and will stop each night and give benefit performances. I urge all of you to come and see these most talented performers and most of all to support the reason for this "Great Trek" — The Damon Runyon Memorial Cancer Fund.

I have been asked to be the "Guiding Star" of this long ride and am delighted to accept.

Warmest Wishes,   JAYNE MANSFIELD

Jayne Mansfield

State of California
GOVERNOR'S OFFICE
SACRAMENTO

EDMUND G. BROWN
GOVERNOR

As Governor of California, I am happy to send the best wishes of the 19 million citizens of this state to the Wranglers on the occasion of their cross-country trip by horseback.

Funds which are received from the trip will be donated to the Damon Runyon Memorial Fund for Cancer Research. The elimination of this blight on our society should be the goal of every American. The research which is carried out under the Damon Runyon Fund is beneficial to all of our citizens, and many of the advances we have made have been derived from the dedicated work of men and women devoted to stamping out cancer in this state and nation.

For these reasons, I am happy to commend the Wranglers on the occasion of this trip. I hope that it will be most successful.

EDMUND G. BROWN, Governor

THE GOVERNOR OF ARIZONA
SAMUEL P. GODDARD

THE CAPITOL
PHOENIX

June 3, 1966

Mr. Marvin Grigsby
General Manager
The Wranglers, Inc.
4224 North 12th Street
Phoenix, Arizona

Dear Mr. Grigsby:

I am pleased to acknowledge and thank you for your letter of April 18 inviting me to participate in the pre-trek program being held in connection with the Damon Runyon Memorial Fund for cancer research.

It is also a pleasure for me to accept your generous invitation to participate in this most worthwhile endeavor. The many wonderful efforts that are expended by so many people in furthering this research can only be repaid by the knowledge that real benefits accrue in the realm of cancer prevention or arrest.

Sincerely,

Goddard
Governor

SG:ds

Letters from the Governors of California and Arizona

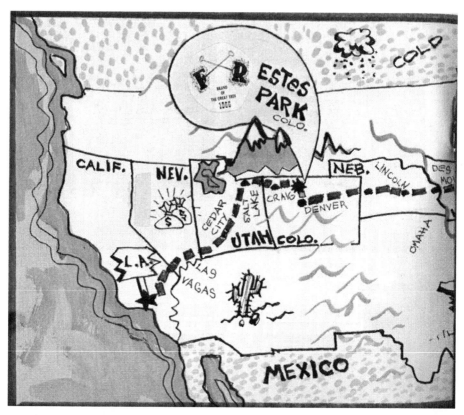

Babe Humphrey   Bob Minser

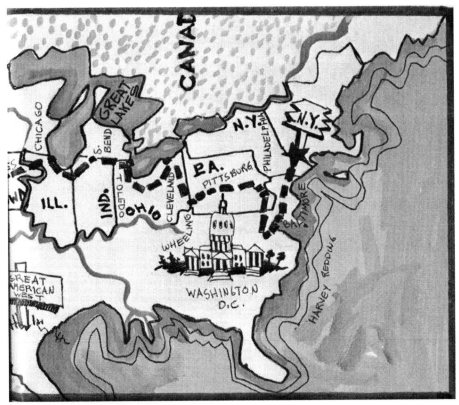

Paul Moyers

Riders on the Chisholm Trail would shudder with shame at the modern machine-age equipment used on The Great Trek of 1966. For instance...

- **The Miley Trailer** transports spare horses, feed and extra track;
- **A Chevrolet** three-quarter ton pick-up, with full air conditioning, pulls the horse trailer;
- **A 1966 Mustang** cruises ahead with the "advance man" to arrange things in towns on the trail;
- **The Clark Cortez House-Car** satisfies the "detail" men;
- **Modern Cameras** Capture exciting moments on the trek;
- **Musical Instruments** by Fender and Kay assure the Wrangler trio their voices reach listeners with fidelity;
- **Levi Clothes**, bearing the trademark of the West, sit astride Porter Saddles and Track for an easier Trek.
- **Gross Suits of Denver**, sharp Western dress for all occasions.

153

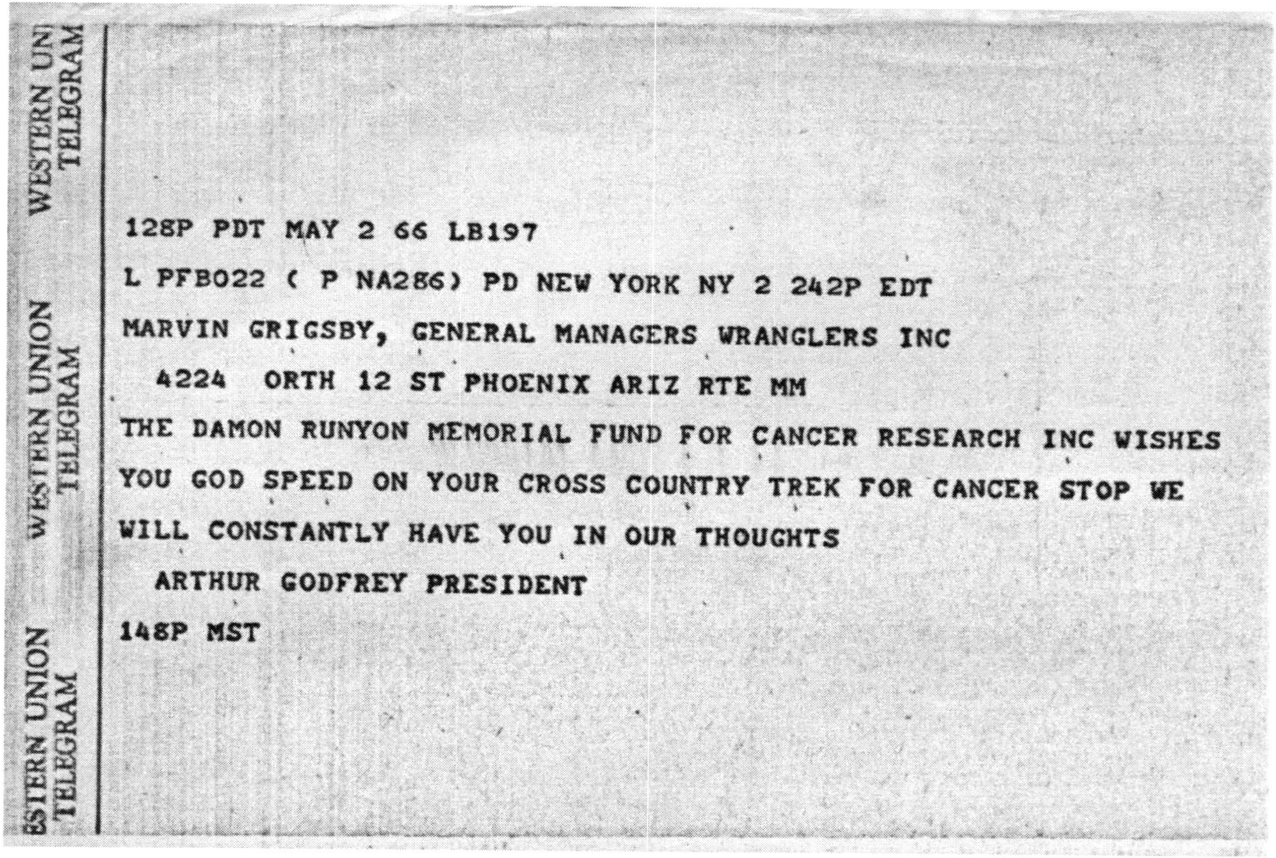

128P PDT MAY 2 66 LB197

L PFB022 (P NA286) PD NEW YORK NY 2 242P EDT

MARVIN GRIGSBY, GENERAL MANAGERS WRANGLERS INC

4224 ORTH 12 ST PHOENIX ARIZ RTE MM

THE DAMON RUNYON MEMORIAL FUND FOR CANCER RESEARCH INC WISHES

YOU GOD SPEED ON YOUR CROSS COUNTRY TREK FOR CANCER STOP WE

WILL CONSTANTLY HAVE YOU IN OUR THOUGHTS

ARTHUR GODFREY PRESIDENT

148P MST

TELEGRAM WESTERN UNION

TELEGRAM WESTERN UNION

TELEGRAM WESTERN UNION

Telegram from Arthur Godfrey

Daily News-Post

and MONROVIA NEWS-POST
JULY 7, 1966 — VOL. 57 — No. 264

—Daily News-Post Photo

Horsemen from Colorado saddle up in Duarte in preparation for a coast-to-coast horseback ride to New York in support of the Damon Runyan Memorial Fund for cancer research. The Estes Park, Colo., men were given a sendoff at the Los Angeles City Hall by city officials and drove to Duarte Wednesday to escape traffic. The "Fall River Wranglers" will perform in major cities along the route to raise money for cancer research. They are (left to right) Babe Humphrey and Paul Moyers, riders; Chuck Kibler, wrangler; and rider Bob Minser. They will arrive in New York Nov. 4, the 20th anniversary of the cancer fund. They expect to ride 31 miles a day.

Wrangler's Camp in Desert

V.F.W. Post to Sponsor The Wranglers Tonight

"The Wranglers"

The Fall River Wranglers in cooperation with the Damon Runyan Memorial Fund for Cancer Research, Inc. will be appearing in St. George at the VFW Patio, Thursday evening, July 21, at 8:30 p. m. Their appearance in St. George is sponsored by the local VFW Post.

The Wranglers will be officially welcomed by Mayor Marion Bowler and the Lions Rodeo Royalty, Miss Gai Reber, 1965 Queen and Shirlee Esplin, 1966 Princess.

The Wranglers are Babe Humphrey, Paul Moyers, and Bob Minser. They are from Estes Park, Colo. and Phoenix, Ariz. They are known as the Fall River Wranglers, because they own a ranch in the Fall River County, in Colo.

They are riding from Los Angeles, Calif. to New York City. They left Los Angeles on July 6—on horseback—to make this trancontinental trek. They will arrive in New York City on November 4, which is the 20th anniversary of the Damon Runyon Memorial Cancer Fund. They ride 30 to 35 miles a day and they will be giving concerts in towns and cities along the way—with the proceeds and donations going to the Cancer Fund.

The Wranglers specialize in Western songs dealing with our great Western Heritage. Their shows are styled for family entertainment.

Admission to the concert is $1.00, proceeds and donations going to the Cancer Fund. Bring the family and enjoy a night of western entertainment.

156

Wranglers ride down center of Cedar City, UT

Wranglers in Vernal, UT - Note: Custom made boots by Tony Lama
Back Left - Rep from Tony Lama Boots

Cortez Motor Home from Clark Equipment

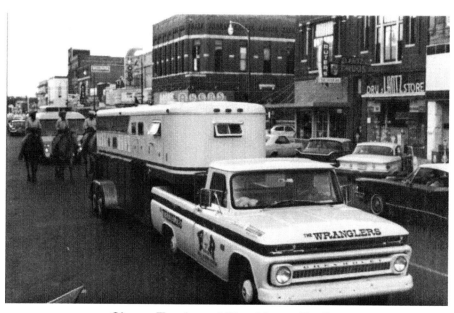

Chevy Truck an Miley Horse Trailer

Cortez Motor Home from Clark Equipment

Chevy Truck an Miley Horse Trailer

Babe with Big Red   Kitty Kibler cleans up after dinner

The sign on the Cortez Motor Home

ESTES PARK TRAIL

VOL. 46. NO. 21   ESTES PARK, COLORADO   FRIDAY, AUG. 19, 1966

THE FALL RIVER WRANGLERS were welcomed by Rodeo Queen Betty Whiteside and some 1,000 other natives and visitors Tuesday as they arrived on "The Great Trek of 1966" for the Damon Runyon Memorial Cancer Fund. Babe Humphrey, Paul Moyers and Bob Minser came into the Village on three of the mounts they are using on their coast-to-coast horseback jaunt. After a parade with the Rooftop Riders, they entertained at Bond Park. That night, they performed for the Fund at the YMCA, the Auditorium and Stanley Hotel.

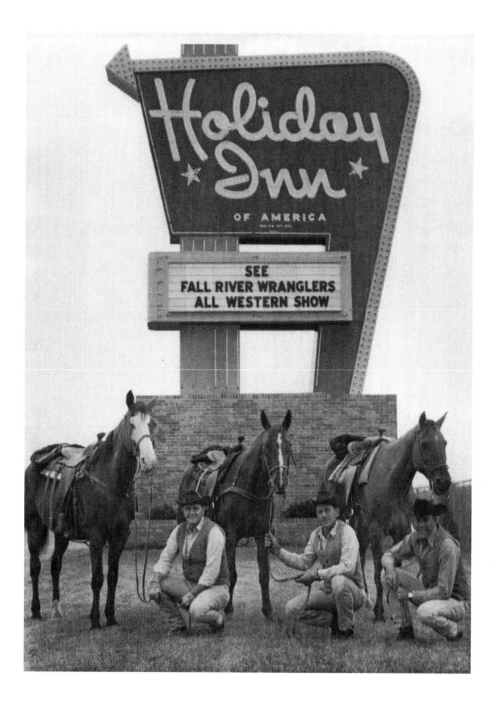

Wranglers at Kearney, NE

Heavy Traffic in Des Moines, September 16

Wranglers to Take Part in Parade Here

An added attraction to the firemen's parade here Saturday night will be the appearance of The Wranglers, a trio of Western TV and recording artists who are on a crosscountry trek to raise money for the Damon Runyon Cancer Memorial.

The Wranglers arrived in Cass county Wednesday and were scheduled to leave the following day on their journey, but have decided to stay over for the firemen's parade.

They will take part in the parade which starts at 8 p.m. Saturday at Second and Chestnut. Following the parade, they will present a 45-minute concert in the city park. A free-will offering will be taken after the concert for the cancer memorial.

Babe Humphrey, Bob Minser and Paul Moyers are The Wranglers and they are accompanied by a crew of five men and a large trailer for their horses. They left on their cross-country trip July 6 and travel about 31 miles daily.

Their stop in Cass county was sponsored by the American Legion and their appearance in the parade is being sponsored by the Rawhiders Saddle club.

Wranglers to Give Concert

The Wranglers, a Western TV and recording group, will appear in the firemen's parade here tomorrow night and then give a 45-minute concert in the city park following the parade. The Wranglers are riding horseback across the country to raise funds for the Damon Runyon Cancer Memorial and are, from the left, Bob Minser, Paul Moyers and Babe Humphrey.

FRIDAY, SEPTEMBER 16, 1966   ATLANTIC NEWS-TELEGRAPH, ATLANTIC, IOWA

By Charles Orman

The "Wranglers," who are on a coast-to-coast horseback ride for the Damon Runyon Memorial Fund for Cancer Research, perform before fora small crowd at the Davenport American Legion hall Friday night. The trio continues its 3,100-mile ride this morning.

2 MORE RUNYON CANCER CONCERTS

Westerners Strum For Fund

By CHARLES ORMAN

Some fine western music was played and sung in Davenport Friday night but only about a dozen persons showed up for the concert at the American Legion Hall.

A second concert was presented later Friday night by the Wranglers at the new Holiday Inn.

The trio from Fall River Ranch, Estes Park, Colo., are riding horseback coast-to-coast promoting the Damon Runyon Memorial Fund for Cancer Research.

The 3,100-mile ride began July 6 at Los Angeles and will end Nov. 4 at the Damon Runyon Memorial Fund 20th anniversary celebration in New York City.

Two more concerts are planned today before the trio heads east. They will appear at McManus Park, Bettendorf, this afternoon and at the Eagle Club, Moline, tonight.

From hilbllly to hymns, the group lives up to its endeavor, "to bring the songs of the West eastward."

The trio, Babe Humphrey, Paul Moyers and Bob Minser, ride 30 to 35 miles a day, giving concerts in towns and cities along the way with the proceeds and donations going to the Damon Runyon Cancer Fund.

1966 NOV 3 PM 2 55

AMA213 (55)(20)LB228

L PFD303 PD 2 EX FAX PHOENIX ARIZ 3 1202P MST

THE WRANGELERS C/O DAMON RUNYON MEMORIAL FUND FOR CANCER RESEARCH

INC.

33 WEST 56 STREET NEW YORK NEW YORK 10019

CONGRATULATIONS ON A SUCCESSFUL CROSS COUNTRY TREK. WHEN ARE

YOU COMING HOME?

KTVK (CHANNEL 3) STAFF PHOENIX ARIZ.

The Fall River Wranglers were officially welcomed by Mayor Marion Bowler and the Lions Rodeo Royalty, Miss Gai Reber, 1965 Queen, and Shirlee Esplin, 1966 Princess. Admission to the concert is $1.00, with proceeds and donations going to the Damon Runyon Cancer Research Foundation. Bring the family and enjoy a night of western entertainment.

I quote this article for a couple of reasons. First, it is similar to all of the articles that were written about the trek. They all told a little about us and what we were doing and where we could be seen. Also, they usually had a photo of us, either with our guitars or on our horses.

The second thing I call to your attention is the price of the show. We didn't make much money for the Cancer Foundation, and maybe we should have charged more, but you must remember that in 1966, gas was about thirty cents a gallon, a good motel room was only five dollars, and you could mail a letter for four cents.

The only money we made on the trip was from selling our records, and we did sell a few of them. This is the money we sent to our families, and each one of us had four kids at home. I would have five before we finished the trek.

A day or two after we left St George, Utah, we arrived in Cedar City, Utah, and were finally out of the triple digit temperatures. It was still hot but not nearly as hot as it had been. We followed I-15 as far north as Provo, Utah, then rode along the Provo River to Heber City, Utah.

It was in Heber City that we got arrested for impersonating ourselves. Someone, I've never found out who, had come to one of our shows and thought we looked too clean and neat to have ridden horses all the way from Los Angeles. He called the sheriff and convinced him that we were fakes. The sheriff took us to jail. The only way we could prove to him that we were who we said we were was to have him call our wives in Colorado and ask them questions about things that only we could know. We finally convinced that sheriff that we were really ourselves, and he let us go with his apologies.

We followed Highway 40 east into Colorado, doing shows in Roosevelt, Utah and Vernal, Utah and reaching Craig, Colorado on the 9th of August.

In Craig we performed a concert at the rodeo grounds prior to the jackpot rodeo. The next night we sang at the Hayden High School gym. We went on to

Steamboat Springs, Colorado and then to Granby, where we left Highway 40 and rode through Rocky Mountain National Park down into Estes Park, Colorado. We had by then traveled about eleven hundred miles and had gone from sea-level to 10,500 feet to boot.

Earlier, I gave warning about riding across the low country in the heat of summer. Now, let me recommend the most beautiful ride you can take in the summer, the one from Steamboat Springs to Estes Park.

Our horses were desert horses, so now we had to get them accustomed to big rocks and tall trees. It's funny what bothers a horse. One thing that really scared them was the big wooden spools that the electric company had left along the side of the road. I had to escort Mare right up to one and let her take a sniff. After she determined that it wasn't going to harm her, she was fine and didn't shy away any more. The tall pines of the Rockies seemed to have the same effect on the horses.

We arrived in Estes Park just in time for me to take Martha to the hospital in Boulder and get back to Estes Park for the first of three performances we had scheduled for that night.

During one of the performances, the president of the Chamber of Commerce surprised me by coming on stage. "Babe, I would like to announce that your wife has just delivered your fifth child and second boy, Bryan. Another future Bar J Wrangler has been born. Mother and baby are doing fine."

Now, I don't want to brag, but you have to admit that the scheduling and execution, and the planning, had to be near perfect in order to pull that off. I can't take all of the credit because Martha did her part too, but I was pretty satisfied with the way things worked out.

We rested for a day or two with our families, then hit the trail again. We headed due east from Estes Park through Greeley and into Fort Morgan, where we followed the route that is now I-76 into Nebraska. An article in the local paper describes our arrival at the northeast corner of Colorado as follows:

The Wranglers, riding horseback from coast to coast for the benefit of cancer research, will gallop into Logan County Friday and stay the weekend. They will stay near Atwood Friday night and ride through Sterling about 9:00 a.m. Saturday. They will continue to Proctor, where they will camp Saturday night. However, they will return to Sterling Saturday night (by car) to give a public performance at the Legion Home from 10:00 to 11:00 p.m. and a private performance (for members only) at the Elks Lodge at 11:00 a.m. Sunday morning. They will continue their trek and will camp at Ovid Sunday night. Monday morning they will head for Brule, Nebraska.

This describes most of the trek. By then the horses and riders were in shape, except for one problem. We didn't figure on gaining weight. Kitty Kibler was too good of a cook, and she was feeding us too well. Kitty cooked two big meals a day, breakfast and dinner. According to a news clipping featuring Kitty, a typical Wrangler breakfast included juice, canned peaches, eggs, sausage, fried potatoes, milk, and coffee.

Kitty reports in the interview, "They'd eat more if I'd fix it. Sometimes I'm making doughnuts at midnight so I'll have something extra to feed them the next morning. Last night I had fried chicken, baked potatoes, tossed salad, creamed corn, and fruit."

Kitty also stated that it wasn't at all unusual for her to stop along the way, whip up a cake, and let it bake in the oven as she cruised down the highway. In addition to her good cooking, she treated us to snacks and lunches as we stopped to perform or to visit with the folks along the way.

As we rode across Nebraska on Route 30, we performed at Ogallala, North Platte, Gothenburg, Lexington, and Kearney, where we did a show at the Holiday Inn. A friend of ours, Bill Beltzer, owned the place. We had been booked there for a time and did a couple of shows while we were there.

By that time, Mare and I were quite the team. I could do about anything I wanted to with her. She followed me everywhere I went if I let her. I taught her to chew gum and often gave her a few sticks. When we got to the Holiday Inn in Kearney, Nebraska I rode her right into the lounge. Everybody got a big kick out of it except maybe Beltzer, who seemed worried about his liquor license or something. I told him not to worry. That I wouldn't give Mare anything stronger than a beer.

Now that I think of it, Beltzer was okay with me riding Mare all over his hotel and actually encouraged us to ride through downtown to promote the shows. He said he would pay for any tickets we got, but I don't remember that we got any.

It was in Nebraska that our advance man Blacky Austin left. Herb Martin met up with us to be our new advance man as we journeyed down the highway somewhere in Nebraska.

By this time, the Fall River Chuckwagon in Estes Park, Colorado had closed for the season, so Jim Dunham, who billed himself as The Gunslinger, the fastest draw in the country, and Lefty Carlson, the trick rope artist at the Fall River Chuckwagon, joined us for the shows while we were in Kearney. Martha and the other wives also came and spent the weekend with us.

After we left Kearney, Mare went lame. Riding down the interstate, which was finished along that stretch, she bruised her cannon bone on a cement spillway that stuck out into the barrow pit. Chuck Kibler did what he could for her but realized that it wasn't enough. She needed a vet.

The vet said that I couldn't ride Mare for a while, so I left her with the vet and bought another horse, this time a Pinto. This slowed us down a bit because the Pinto wasn't in shape. We made it work for the next month or so until Mare healed, and I sent the trailer back to pick her up. We kept the Pinto, so then we had two spares. We rested the horses more often after that.

When we arrived in Lincoln, Nebraska, we went right by the capitol. We came upon a big fountain near the capitol, and the horses all had a drink. We got a couple of funny looks, but nobody said anything. The capitol in Lincoln is unique in that it is one of only two United States capitols that does not have a dome.

We did a couple of shows in the Lincoln area, and then it was off to Omaha. From Omaha we angled northeast into Iowa through the town of Oakland, Iowa, where we did one show and moved on to Atlantic, Iowa, where we did a couple of shows. After Atlantic, we picked up I-80, which was almost complete, and went on to Des Moines.

As we rode, the things we found on the highway were kind of funny. We found several wallets, one that had been lost for over three years. We found all types of clothing. Back in 1966, not all cars had air conditioning. Folks drove with their windows down, and clothes blew off hangers and out windows. The funniest thing we found was a suit coat. About five miles down the road, we found the pants that matched the coat. Unfortunately the suit didn't fit any of us, so we tossed it in the box we had set aside for all the stuff we found.

We arrived in Des Moines, Iowa, on September 18th. We rode right down main street during rush hour. Folks honked and waved at us, and a few who thought that we were really remarkable showed their rabid admiration by holding up their thumbs, signifying to us that we were number one, at least in their minds.

By then, the horses were used to cars and crowds, and virtually nothing fazed them. After Des Moines, we did shows in Newton, Grinnell, Davenport, and Bettendorf, Iowa. On September 24th, we crossed the Mississippi River and did a show in Moline, Illinois. We followed I-80 to Chicago, doing shows as we went. I have a clipping that says we were in Ottawa, Illinois, on September 29th.

As I described earlier, we were often met by a welcoming committee of local riding clubs that escorted us through town, but in Chicago we were greeted by a different type of welcoming committee than we were used to. We rode right down Cicero Avenue, which was one of the main streets through Chicago, and came upon an elementary school where the kids were out playing at recess. When those kids saw our horses, they poured into the street and surrounded us. We stopped the horses and quieted them the best we could as the kids hugged and petted them. There must have been four hundred children, and I was scared to death. The horses stood quiet as the kids milled around them until some teachers saw what was going on and rescued us. Thankfully, no one got hurt. The kids returned to the school yard, and we went on our way. If this had happened earlier on our ride, I hate to think what might have happened.

By that time, though, the horses were so used to us that if we didn't seem upset they didn't get upset either. Mare trusted me completely, and I could take her anywhere. I mentioned previously how I had ridden her into the Holiday Inn in Kearney. I don't think I shared that I put her in the elevator and took her up to my room. She went anywhere I wanted her to go.

While we were in Chicago, we did a guest segment on Dolph Huit's Chicago Barn Dance. Dolph had come up with the idea for the Chicago Barn Dance TV show, and our advance man had contacted Dolph to let him know that we would be in the area. The show went over so well that he booked us to do a whole show after we completed the ride.

As we rode across Indiana, two interesting things happened. First, we picked up a new member of the group, a dog we called Rusty. Rusty began following us soon after we crossed into Indiana. At first we threw clods of dirt and rocks at him to try to get him to go home, but after three days, he was still with us. He stayed just out of range of the rocks and clods but wouldn't leave. We finally fed him, and he became a permanent member of our gang. He trotted beside us, and if the road was narrow, he got right underneath a horse and jogged right with it.

The other thing that happened was that we got acquainted with some Amish folks, and they introduced us to boron carbide. The Amish, who used horses on paved roads, had found that if they spot-welded boron carbide on the horses' shoes, it cut down on the horse slipping on the pavement. We got a supply of it and used it for the rest of the trip. It worked like a charm. I wish we had known about it earlier.

One problem I had in Indiana was that Mare was scared to death of the black Amish buggies we passed on the highway. I guess she thought that this square black thing was chasing other horses down the road, and she wanted no part of them. Unlike the wooden spools, she never did get used to the one-horse buggies.

On the 16th of October, we rode into Bowling Green, Ohio, where we promptly got arrested again. It seems that one of the horses left a deposit on the street, and a deputy arrested us for littering. He sort of

3 Horsemen Pushing Cancer Fund Jailed

BOWLING GREEN, Ohio, Oct. 17—(UPI)—Three horsemen from Estes Park, Colo., were jailed Sunday night here for "littering" because one of their horses was too messy.

The three, riding horseback from Los Angeles to New York to promote the Damon Runyon Cancer Fund, are Babe Humphrey, Paul Moyers and Bob Minser. They are to appear at the annual Harvest Moon Ball Nov. 4 at New York City to help begin the yearly cancer fund drive.

The ride is in commemoration of the 20th anniversary of the death of Damon Runyon, former Denver, Pueblo, Colo., and New York newspaperman who died of cancer.

reminded me of Barney Fife, the Don Knotts character on the Andy Griffith show.

I could smell a good story, so we went into court and pleaded not guilty. The arresting office had apparently been shipped off to somewhere else, so he was unavailable to testify. The media in town picked up on the story, as I hoped it would, and we got in the papers and on the news. More publicity for the trek.

The judge, thoroughly embarrassed at this unusual turn of events, changed our plea to guilty, suspended our fine, and ordered us to get out of town lickety-split. He was none too happy that the town had been made to look so foolish.

We left Bowling Green with our heads held high and made for Pennsylvania. Crossing Pennsylvania went smoothly, and we rode into New Jersey. Patterson, New Jersey, was the last stop before we entered New York City. We had arrived on time, and all we had to do was cross the George Washington Bridge. As we rode up to the bridge, the horses balked and wouldn't move. The problem was that the expansion joints in the bridge looked like cattle guards to the horses, and they wouldn't budge. We had an escort of various police vehicles, we were holding up traffic, and things were falling apart fast. Finally, we unloaded Big Red from the trailer and led him across the joints. He wasn't spooked by them as he was the old horse of the bunch and had been around more than the others had. Thankfully, when the other horses saw that Red could do it, they followed, and we rode into New York City, thirty-one hundred miles after we had begun the trek in Los Angeles.

The Damon Runyon people put us in a place called Forest Hills, where we had room for the motor home and the horse trailer and the rest of our entourage.

On the evening of November 4, 1966, at 7:30 p.m., we attended the 20th Anniversary Dinner Dance of the Damon Runyon Cancer Research Foundation at The Rainbow Room in the RCA Building, 30 Rockefeller Plaza, and presented a representative of the Foundation with the money we had raised along the way. Unfortunately, it wasn't much after our expenses were taken out, but the Damon Runyon Foundation did get good publicity from the adventure.

Martha, Bob Minser's wife, and Herb Martin's wife joined us in New York for the presentation. We all sat at one table by ourselves, so none of the western would rub off on any of the paying guests. It was a black tie affair, and someone told us that there wasn't a woman in the room who was wearing a dress that had cost less than five thousand dollars. That didn't include the women at our table, however. We sang three or four songs, all of which earned us hearty applause.

We got to meet Arthur Godfrey and some of the other dignitaries. There were over four hundred people in attendance, but not as many as we were used to feeding at the Fall River Chuckwagon, or any of the other Chuckwagons with which I had been associated, for that matter.

We looked around New York City for a day or two and then headed west. Chuck and Kitty took the horses back to Scottsdale with them, our wives flew home, and Bob, Paul, and I rode home in the Mustang. We carried our instruments with us as we had the show to do in Chicago and the one we had booked in Green Bay, Wisconsin.

We each kept our own horses in the end, and I took Rusty home with me where he lived with us for several years until he died. Though I'm glad we completed the trek, financially it wasn't what we had hoped for.

I think the biggest reason why we didn't raise more money was because the Damon Runyon people dropped the ball on advertising and promotion. They simply didn't get the word out on the national press like they said they would. Because of that, when we rode into a town, the only way that folks knew that we were coming was because our advance man had told them. Blacky and Herb did a superior job, but this didn't pack the punch that the national news would have delivered if a crowd had been following us as was originally planned.

I guess we got some publicity from the trek, but I doubt it sold many Chuckwagon tickets for us. One thing is for sure, darn few people can say that they have ridden horseback across the United States, and it is something I will never forget.

Chapter Eight

BACK TO COLORADO

After the trek ended on November 4, 1966, Bob and I went home to Colorado Springs. Paul and his wife were having some problems, so Paul went to California. Unfortunately, the trek had left us nearly broke. I went back to KPIK radio as a disk jockey for two or three months so I could put some food on the table.

About that time, Frank Vale asked me if I would be willing to come back to the Lazy B Chuckwagon the next summer and help out and create a new and better show. Tom Justin had been managing it, but Frank felt that Tom's lack of know-how in some areas was keeping the operation from being all that it could be.

Lazy B Wranglers
LR - Bob Minser, Tom Justin, Babe Humphrey

Needless to say, I was dumbfounded when Frank Vale approached me with the idea of going back to the Lazy B. But he apologized profusely for way he had handled things before. We had several lengthy discussions about his proposal.

Now, this may sound screwed up to you. It sure did to me, and I questioned whether it could possibly work. But after visiting with Tom, I decided that it might. I had a soft spot in my heart for the Lazy B. After all, I had built it and hated to see it fail. I didn't necessarily trust Frank, but since I had feelings for the Lazy B, I agreed to go back.

Tom was a capable guy, but he knew he needed some help. I provided some assistance and made a few suggestions here and there. I got the music arranged so Tom could sing the lead, and Bob Minser and I sang the harmony. I worked hard with Tom to get a fantastic show up and running.

Bob and I went to Scottsdale and got Mare and Chaw, our trek horses, and put them in a corral for everyone to see. We put up a sign at the Lazy B telling the story of the trek. The horses loved the attention they got at the Lazy B.

We still had to find something to do in the winter. In late 1966, I contacted Jim Sheldon, who scheduled

USO shows, and told him that we wanted to do a USO show. Bob Minser, Tom Justin, and I auditioned for Jim in Denver, and he hired us to do a twenty-two-day show on the hospital circuit in the Pacific. He told us that we had to take a girl performer with us as the troops liked to see a girl in the show.

He assigned Janie Davids to go with us. She was a western singer and a yodeler who played the guitar and the banjo. She had had her own TV show for ten months on ABC in Los Angeles. She had records out and had performed in Las Vegas and at Lake Tahoe. This was her second USO tour, so she was the veteran in the group. She wasn't on stage during all of the time that we were, but she did three or four numbers. We backed her up while she performed.

The tour took us to all the Far East islands beginning with Tokyo. We visited Wake, Guadalcanal, the Philippines, and Guam to name a few. I had the rating of a GS-15. This was a civilian status ranking system used by the federal government. A GS-15 was about the same as a full bird Colonel, so I had a little pull at my disposal. I used it while we visited Guam to get my younger brother, Dean, who was stationed in

USO Show Poster
Top - Janie Davids, Lower LR - Tom Justin, Babe, Bob Minser

Guam, a three-day pass to come and hear us play and to chat with me while we were there.

Another thing I did during the summer of 1967 in Estes Park to help pay the bills was to do some radio work for a brand new station that had just gone on the air KKEP. A Denver radio station wanted to have a presence in Estes Park, so I was hired to do some sports announcing and programming. I also played the good old western music that folks enjoyed listening to. I had a chance to talk up the Lazy B Chuckwagon and invite the listeners to come out for supper and the show.

I traveled with the high school football and basketball teams announcing and doing the play-by-play broadcasts for them. This was a new thing for me, but I loved sports, and it was fun.

Tom Justin, Bob Minser, Larry Steel, and I took a trip to Nashville that winter. Larry Steel, a songwriter with a good voice, wanted us to back him up and play for him while he cut a couple of 45 records for the K-Arc Label. We sang some harmony and some ooh-aahs, and he recorded *Hard Times* and other songs. While we were there, we worked with additional artists doing the same thing. Thus, we made some money, which helped out. As before, there were those in Nashville who really wanted us to stay, but as I expressed earlier, I wanted my own place, and I wanted to be home every night. We came home. Larry never sang at the Chuckwagon with us as he preferred country music to the western songs that we sang.

The spring of 1968 found us preparing for another year at the Lazy B when I received two phone calls that changed our plans.

The first one was from Russ Wolfe at the Flying W Chuckwagon. "Say, Babe, Cy is leaving the Flying W to open his own place in Durango, Colorado. I need someone to take over the Flying W Wranglers, along with other management chores, for me. I'm serving twelve hundred guests a night, and I need someone who knows what he's doing. Could you come down and give me a hand?"

"Let me think it over, Russ. I'll get back to you." My mouth hung open in astonishment.

At this same time, Frank Vale called and requested that I come to his office for a visit. "Babe, I have a letter here that I want you to give to Tom Justin. The letter states that Tom is no longer the manager of the Lazy B and that you will be assuming the position of manager."

Now Tom and I were good friends, and he had done everything I had asked him to do the previous year. I told Martha that I just couldn't do that to Tom.

I was frustrated with the Chuckwagon business. I wanted my own place, I wasn't getting it, and I didn't have enough money to get it. I was down in the dumps.

This last trick of Frank's helped me make up my mind, and I spoke to Frank. "Frank, I quit. This is the second time that you have pulled something like this on me. You should keep Tom on as manager. He is more capable of doing a good job than he was before I spent last summer with him. Good luck."

I knew that I could work for Russ and be content, so I met with him and took the job. As I remember, he agreed to all of my requests. I told Bob Minser what I planned to do and that he had a job if he wanted it.

Bob wanted to sing with us, but before we opened, he got a call from the Sons Of The Pioneers. They offered him a job singing with them. He asked me what I thought, and I told him that he had better take the job because it sounded like a better deal than he had with me. He went to sing with the Sons. He only stayed with them for a few months because he couldn't record with them, due to the judge's order that I referred to earlier.

If he had recorded with them, they would have lost the right to retain their name. Without getting a cut of their record money and the notoriety of being on the label with them, Bob got discouraged and left. He eventually went to work for Cy down in Durango where he sang until he retired.

Having returned to the Flying W Chuckwagon to manage the new show, it was a challenge to find the talent needed to entertain twelve hundred people a night in a very short amount of time.

I remembered that my younger brother Larry could play the upright bass and could also sing. He could also hear all the parts necessary for singing four- and five-part harmonies, which we did frequently, one person singing more than one part.

I called Larry. "Hey, I need some help here at the Flying W Chuckwagon. Would you be interested in being a Flying W Wrangler for a spell?"

Fortunately for me, he said that he would do it. I still had to find two more singers and a fiddle player. I had known Larry Morgan for years and knew that he would be an asset to the group if I could convince him to join us. I remember him telling me that he wasn't sure if he could do all that I wanted him to do, but with a bit of persuasion and my assurance that plenty of rehearsals would get him ready, he agreed to give it a go.

I still needed another singer and a good fiddle player.

As fate would have it, while fixing fence one day at the Flying W Ranch, a car pulled up and out stepped a fellow named Sam Nichola. "Are you by any chance looking for a good fiddle player?"

"Maybe. How about you come to my house tonight for a practice session with the trio, and we'll see how you do?" I couldn't believe my luck.

"I can't sing worth a darn, but I can play anything that you can sing," Sam replied, quite confident.

That was good enough for me. That was in 1968, and Sam stayed at the Flying W Chuckwagon for thirty odd years fiddling with various Flying W Wrangler groups. He was loyal, always on time, and never missed a night playing the fiddle. Sam retired from the Flying W Chuckwagon and sadly passed away in 2008. I am honored to have played music with Sam for years at the Flying W and various other shows, including a USO show in Vietnam. Sam was a good friend, and he will be missed. We still needed another singer and a funny man, and J.B. Tankersly filled the bill. J.B. worked as a ranch hand at the Flying W Ranch, could play guitar, and could sing the lead part. He rounded out our first five performers in 1968.

We rehearsed every night to get the show ready for our first summer on stage. We found that our voices blended well. We were all nervous that first night as we kicked off our 1968 season. The show sold out, and the crowd cheered. I breathed a huge sigh of relief.

I stayed at the Flying W Chuckwagon for ten more years and mastered important skills in managing food preparation, promotion, and convention booking. I will always be thankful for my time there with Russ Wolfe and his family. The enormous number of things I learned there helped me in my endeavor to own and run my own family Chuckwagon. Besides organizing the show and hiring new entertainers, there were other duties and responsibilities and interesting events that took place during this time. I had to make sure that I had cooks lined up and that I had as many others as it would take to prepare food for twelve hundred people, serve it to them, and then to clean up afterwards.

Back then, we cooked with slabs for heat that we carried in from the sawmill. Slabs were cut from trees when they were squared up to be cut up into dimensional lumber. The Indians handled the slabs and got them burning each night.

After dinner the Indian boys changed into their native costumes and danced in the show. The Indians pleased the audience with their native dances, which were educational as well. Joe David Marcas' hoop and eagle dance was the finest I have ever seen. He also

Flying W Wranglers, Babe & Larry Humphrey & Taos Indian Dancers

performed the Lord's Prayer in sign language while we sang it during the inspirational portion of the show. Sonny Montoya danced with Joe David, and while they danced, Mike Concha chanted.

* * *

Mike Concha and I were about the same age, so we had quite a bit in common. We became good friends. When his wife Sally went home to visit her family, he got lonely and came over to the house in the middle of the night.

He stood out on the lawn and called to me, "Mr. Hummeries, Mr. Hummeries. Let's chant."

I invariably got out of bed, went outside to get him, and brought him into the house before he woke up the whole neighborhood and someone called the police. I sat him at the kitchen table, and he chanted some more. We used the kitchen table for the drum. I got him to teach me the authentic Indian chanting songs, and I chanted with him in harmony for hours at a time. We also wore out a kitchen table or two. Martha lay in bed and listened to us chant. Like I said, Martha has put up with a lot.

Mike left the Flying W about the same time as I did in 1977 and returned to Taos, New Mexico, where he eventually became Governor of the Taos Tribe of Indians. I kind of lost track of him over the years but have had news of him through a mutual friend, Glenna Gieck. I know that he is well. I have precious memories of Mike and his family.

* * *

The guys and I put the show together and had a fine summer. We were back in Colorado Springs, the kids were in school, and we could finally start living like a normal family. My salary as manager was paid for the entire year, so we didn't need to worry about starving during the winter months.

I traveled around the area talking to motel and hotel owners and putting out brochures advertising the Flying W Chuckwagon. I also called on places that held conventions in the area and tried to convince them to send their guests to spend one night of their stay in Colorado Springs at the Flying W. After I had done this for a year or two, several of the local attractions broke away from the Chamber of Commerce and formed an association known as the Pike's Peak Region Attractions Association. The Flying W Chuckwagon was one of them, along with Garden of the Gods, Santa's Workshop, The Royal Gorge, and several others.

PIKES PEAK REGION ATTRACTIONS ASSOCIATION

1050 SOUTH 21ST STREET ● COLORADO SPRINGS, COLORADO 80904

FOR IMMEDIATE RELEASE:

Contact George Pederson, 303-633-7325

The Pikes Peak Pied Piper was in _____ recently.

Babe Humphrey, known as the Pikes Peak Pied Piper visited_____ giving travel tips and telling everyone about Pikes Peak Country in Colorado. He is one of four individuals currently travelling some 16,000 miles throughout the mid-west as goo will ambassadors of tourism in the Pikes Peak area.

Humphrey, who is a cowboy, singer and foreman of the Flying W Ranch in Colorado Springs, is travelling extensively in Texas and Oklahoma as a Pied Piper.

The Pied Piper project was brought about when a gas crisis hit Colorado Springs early in the summer of 1973. That year the Pied Piper went into five states to tell the vacationers there was a plentiful supply of gasoline. Since then, the program has grown to include 17 states covering some 16,000 miles. Scheduled stops for the Pied Pipers include Dallas, Houston, Oklahoma City, Omaha, Des Moines Detroit, Chicago, Minneapolis/St Paul, St. Louis and approximately 150 other cities throughout the mid-west.

Each of the Pikes Peak Pied Pipers tell vacation-minded individuals how to plan for their vacation to have more fun, yet spend less money.

"The success of the Pied Piper is based on the credibility of the message," Humphrey said recently in an interview. "We feel that everyone would like to know what we have to offer in Pikes Peak Country and we're proud of the product."

In travelling through the mid-west, Humphry said, "it is a good feeling to talk and visit with so many people. But most of all, everyone who has ever visited our area has nothing but good things to say about it. And when you have a product of that nature, it isn't difficult to sell."

-30-

Pied Piper Letter

The new Association hired me to do for them what I had been doing for the Flying W, with Russ's blessing. They gave me the name of The Pied Piper.

With the added expense money and a larger budget, I decided to go into all of the mid-west states and Texas. Now, instead of getting folks to come to the Flying W Chuckwagon while they were in the area, I enticed them to come to the area itself by showing them all of the attractions for tourists in the Colorado Springs area. I went on television in the cities I visited and worked with groups to try to persuade them to have their conventions in Colorado Springs. This also helped me in my future life, especially when I eventually owned my own Chuckwagon in Jackson Hole, Wyoming.

During the winter in early 1970, we decided to do another USO tour. I had another chat with Jim Sheldon. "Jim, I'd like to do another tour, but I have a different group of entertainers with me this time. Would that work for you?"

"Babe, if you say they can sing, that's good enough for me. You did a good job last time. And, Babe, you don't need to worry about taking a girl this time. Where would you like to go?"

"How about Vietnam?" I answered.

COMING SOON! | **VIETNAM THAILAND** | CONTACT YOUR SPECIAL SERVICES OFFICER FOR DETAILS

2nd USO Tour
LR - Larry Humphrey, Babe Humphrey, Sam Nichola,
Larry Morgan, JB Tankersley

The tour was set for February of 1970, and the group was to go to Vietnam and Thailand. We set about getting all of the paperwork done and getting the numerous vaccinations that were required to go into that part of the world. We got vaccinated for everything from the flu to the plague.

When the five of us finally got to Vietnam, we were assigned to the third floor of the Mirachord Hotel in Saigon. This is where all of the USO people stayed. Captain Dutko was our escort officer and was responsible for getting us where we needed to go. He was also responsible for our safety.

The guys and I were scheduled to play at all the Officers' Clubs and some hospitals, but I had a discussion with Captain Dutko. "We want to entertain the grunts and the troops on the line. The actual fighting men need the entertainment. We want to go into the interior and really entertain the troops."

"That's too dangerous. Mr. Humphrey. If you want to do that, you'll have to sign a release holding the United States government harmless if any of you get hurt." He spoke in a business-like way.

I signed the document, and next thing I knew, we were on gun boats and helicopters in the middle of the

Vietnam War. One of the places we went was called Fire Base Buttons, which was an outpost in the jungle surrounded by communists. Fire Base had a howitzer that rotated in a circle, firing a barrage every three minutes to protect the base. Only one-fourth of the troops on the base could attend the show while the other three-fourths were sent out to the perimeter of the base to protect us during our show and our time on the base. I don't know who decided who would watch the show and who would defend. There may have been some sort of lottery system.

Another unit we visited was really out of the way. It was an advanced recon out-post of sixty troops, and no one wanted to fly us in because there were enemy ground-to-air missiles in that area. Finally one helicopter pilot said he would do it. The technique he used was to fly high over the jungle and then to descend rapidly in an evasive landing procedure. He spun the helicopter as he descended. The centrifugal force while dropping pinned us to the walls of the helicopter.

He put us down, and we did the show, but then nobody wanted to fly in and pick us up. Finally some old boy from Tennessee heard about us, and because he really liked western music, he volunteered to pick us up. His conditions were that only the five of us could get on the helicopter due to weight issues. No equipment, instruments, or anything else but us. He came in and landed, and we jumped on. He was in the air again in less than three minutes. Our escort officer was not happy. He had to stay with our equipment and ride back to Saigon through the jungle in a truck.

Another time we flew into a prison camp on a two-engine plane, and one of the motors quit. The pilot radioed ahead that we had a problem but told us that he hoped he could land okay. It didn't help much that we could see the runway and all of the fire trucks that scrambled to get into position to put out the fire in case we crashed. The pilot made a perfect landing just as he hoped he would.

One funny thing happened when we took a day off and went to the beach to do some swimming. Sam, floating on an air mattress, drifted into an area where the sewer from the base dumped into the ocean. We tried to get him out of there, but he didn't pay any attention to us and thought we were just fooling around. When he finally found out that we were on the level, he got mad. We teased him about that for a long time.

Another incident involved my brother, Larry Humphrey, and Larry Morgan. We had an afternoon off in a town close to the territory controlled by the North Vietnamese. In fact, half of the town was in the north and half in the south. It was safe enough to be there, but it was too close for my comfort. Anyway, the two Larry's found their way into a bar and imbibed a bit. Then Larry Humphrey discovered that his wallet was missing. I had gone looking for them and happened into the Bar Just as they had lined up nine Vietnamese and the bartender against the wall to be searched in an effort to find Larry's wallet.

Confusion reigned as neither party could speak the other's language. As it turned out, all of us were wearing fatigues with several pockets on the leg, and when I brushed up against Larry, I felt his wallet in a pocket on the leg of his fatigues. I marched the Larrys out of the bar and back to the hotel with Larry Humphrey protesting and justifying his actions, saying that the Vietnamese would have stolen his wallet it if they had been given half a chance.

Their drinking also got us in trouble in Thailand, where we visited some hospitals and a couple of bases. I was in my room one night when the whole floor of our hotel was awakened by the two Larrys shouting at each other. I got up and went down the hall to see what was wrong. Larry Humphrey pounded on the door for Larry Morgan to open the door. Morgan yelled back at him that he had hunted all over the room and couldn't find the key. My brother shouted at Morgan that he didn't need a key. He just needed to open the door!

Department of Defense

United States Military Assistance Command, Vietnam

Certificate of Appreciation

is awarded to

BABE HUMPHREY

FOR YOUR OUTSTANDING CONTRIBUTION TO THE MORALE AND WELFARE OF THE UNITED STATES AND OTHER FREE WORLD MILITARY ASSISTANCE FORCES IN THE REPUBLIC OF VIETNAM WHILE TOURING THE COMMAND, ENTERTAINING PERSONNEL OF ALL SERVICES. THE SIGNIFICANT AND LASTING IMPRESSION YOU MADE ENHANCED THE MORALE OF THE FIGHTING FORCES AND REFLECTS GREAT CREDIT UPON YOURSELF AND YOUR PROFESSION.

SAIGON, VIETNAM

Date   7 February 1970

CREIGHTON W. ABRAMS
General, United States Army

USARV 1850/9 (11-68)

Certificate of Appreciation from the Department of Defense

LR- JB Tankersly, Capt. Dutko, Larry Humphrey, Gen. Abrams
Babe Humphrey, Sam Nichola, Larry Morgan

* * *

We returned to Colorado Springs on schedule with
no more excitement and prepared for our next season at
the Flying W Chuckwagon. About six weeks later, we
heard that the Mirachord Hotel in Saigon where we had
stayed had been leveled in an explosion, claiming many
lives.

In 1971, during my third or fourth year at the
Flying W, I convinced Russ that we should build a
steakhouse restaurant so we would have something to

do in the winter. This would help me keep the entertainers together and give them something to do in the off season. All of them had full time jobs somewhere else, but my hope was that we could do enough business that they could just entertain for a living. It took us over a year to build the steakhouse, but we got it done and did two seatings every Friday and Saturday night.

The guys helped serve, and after dinner we entertained. We opened the steakhouse on weekends in the wintertime, except during the months of January and February, when everyone took time off for vacation.

The steakhouse did a good business. Like at the Chuckwagon, the wranglers were the waiters, so the customers enjoyed a closeness with the entertainers.

One time a good friend of Russ Wolfe's called and said that he wanted to bring a dozen folks to dinner. Russ told me that his friend was a wine connoisseur and wanted to bring his own bottles rather than serve the California brand that we had. He said that his friend would drop off several bottles of the wine early in the afternoon so that it would have time to chill properly for the evening meal.

I was really busy when the friend dropped off the wine, and somehow I completely forgot to put it in the cooler to chill. I decided that I would have to speed the process up, so I threw the wine into the freezer, hoping that I could play catch up and still have the wine ready. When I went back to check on the wine, I found that it had frozen, and all of the bottles were broken. I hurriedly called the liquor store seeking replacements, only to find out that the label sold for over one hundred dollars a bottle and that it wasn't available in Colorado Springs at any cost. It was an imported wine not stocked in Colorado Springs.

It was now my painful duty to inform the boss of what I had done. When I looked around, I found that all the other guys had disappeared, and I had to face Russ by myself. Russ grinned and called his friend and told him what had happened. His friend laughed and said that he had a few more bottles at home and would bring them and not to worry about it.

This is the kind of guy Russ Wolfe was. He handled the big crises better than the small ones. This was a good lesson for me, and I've put it to use several times since. Things like that are going to happen occasionally, and when they do, the best way to handle them is head on and honestly.

* * *

We were always building something at the Flying W Ranch. We built Irene's Homestead, which served as a gift shop. We built a walk-in freezer so we could keep more meat on hand. We put down thousands of brick pavers so the customers would have an easier time roaming around on the property. We built a western town, which was a good money-maker. Most of the customers came early and wandered around the town for an hour or more before supper and the show. Each building they entered served as a revenue source, and the Flying W flourished.

In the early seventies, I heard about a young singer who performed in a bar in Colorado Springs. I stopped in to listen to him and was impressed with his voice but not particularly with his appearance. He was a hippy type with long hair who liked to sing songs he had written while in Nashville.

I listened for a while, and when he had finished his set, I invited him to my table and introduced myself. "Scott, my name is Babe Humphrey. I run the Flying W

Chuckwagon. I sing with a group of Wranglers there. Have you ever heard of it?"

"No."

"Maybe you'd like to come and check it out. Have you ever considered singing to a sober audience?" I got right down to business.

He grinned. "Ya, okay. I'll come and take a look."

This was the first time that Scotty Vaughn had ever been to a Chuckwagon, but it certainly wouldn't be the last. He decided that it might be a good place to work, and we changed a hippy into a cowboy singer. He replaced Larry Morgan and became a mainstay at the Flying W Chuckwagon. He also spent some time with me after I opened "The Bar-J Chuckwagon" in Jackson Hole, Wyoming.

During the last four or five years, Scott felt God pulling and directing him. He began a ministry through song and the spoken word around the country. He's given up the applause for the pulpit and is leading all who will come to Jesus. What a turnaround! He is such an exceptional witness, and I can't tell you how impressed I am with his commitment to Christ. I am so pleased for him, and he will surely have his reward in Heaven.

All of the Wranglers had a great camaraderie and were always pulling practical jokes on each other. One of the best of these happened up at the Lazy B after I left there. It was so good and so typical of the stuff that went on that I want to include it here. Jim Dunham tells the story this way.

One of the things we did to save money was to eat at the Chuckwagon most nights, although the menu never changed. You had to eat out to get some variety.

Tom Justin hired a young fellow named Jeff from the hills of Tennessee to sing tenor and play guitar. Jeff was friendly but was always kind of down. One day he showed up wearing a big smile. I asked him what had caused the change, and he said that he missed his girl back home, but he had proposed to her over the phone. She was going to come to Estes Park after Labor Day, and they were going to get married. To save money, Jeff ate every meal at the Chuckwagon for the next one hundred days. He ate the same beef, beans, and biscuits each day.

The whole band attended the wedding, and following the show that evening, the newlyweds hopped into a horse-drawn wagon and headed off to start their honeymoon.

As the rest of us cleaned tables and picked up trash, which was part of our jobs in those days, Lynn Campbell said, "Jeff doesn't have to stay late and clean up tonight."

Tom commented, "And he doesn't have to eat beef and beans again tonight!"

Brian Davies asked, "I wonder where he's going?"

I thought for a moment and said, "I know where he's going!"

Jeff had asked me for a recommendation for a romantic restaurant and a place to stay since he knew that I was familiar with the local places. I had recommended the Glen Haven Inn, a fabulous place that served gourmet meals and had beautiful accommodations. Mr. And Mrs. Wells, who owned the lodge, were nationally known chefs, and some of the items on the menu had to be ordered at least four hours ahead as they were custom prepared.

I immediately rushed into the Lazy B kitchen and asked Helen if we had any beef and beans left.

"Yes, but they don't look all that appetizing."

"Don't worry about that. Can you make me up two Chuckwagon suppers on tin plates?" I queried in a big hurry.

I then jumped into my car and raced down the back road to Glen Haven. I got to the Inn before Jeff and his bride did since they had to switch from the horse-drawn buggy to an automobile.

I took my two plates into Mrs. Wells' kitchen. "I know you have prepared cordon bleu for our friends, and I don't want you to not serve that. But before you do, and just after the salad and the wine, would you mind placing these two plates on the table in front of the bride and groom to see what their reaction is?"

The boys had followed me and hid in the back room as Mrs. Wells set the tin plates in front of the couple. Jeff took one look and couldn't believe his eyes.

He put his head in his hands. "Oh, my God. Oh, my God. Oh my God..."

Most of our pranks were nowhere near this elaborate. But I sure wish I had been there to see that one.

* * *

I got a phone call in the early seventies from Dale Warren of the Sons Of The Pioneers. He wanted to know

212

if I would come to California to consult with them about opening up a Chuckwagon there. I met with Dale, Rusty Richards, Luther Nallie, and Gary Lemaster. We went to the location they had picked out, which was north of San Francisco in the Redwoods, to look things over. I spent three days with them going over what I thought they should know to make a successful venture out of it. They agreed with every thing I told them until we got to the alcohol issue.

The Son's themselves were fine with it, but the guy who owned the building in which they wanted to put the Chuckwagon had never heard of a steakhouse or a show of this kind that didn't serve booze. He insisted that one had to sell booze. I maintained that to make it work and have the show be a family show, alcohol couldn't be part of it. I guess they must have believed that I knew what I was talking about, and I guess that their partner wouldn't change his mind because they never opened the Chuckwagon. It's a shame that they didn't because I think with the location they had and the show they could have offered, they would have made a success of it.

And then there was the time at the Flying W Chuckwagon in the winter of 1973 when I broke my ring finger on my left hand. That might not seem like a big deal to some, but to a guitar player, it could be a career-ending injury. We had been working on the outside stage area, raising the floor, putting on a rain cover to protect the mikes and instruments in case of a storm, just generally overhauling our show area to make it a nicer place in which to entertain an outside audience. If we knew it was going to storm, we did the show inside the building, but once in a while a stray cloud floated in and gave us a surprise shower. Rain on microphones can also be a career-ending catastrophe, much worse than a broken finger.

We had just finished the floor and started on the stage covering. A wooden beam about a foot in diameter and twenty feet long needed to be taken down and moved higher. We had it loosened up and ready to move when it slipped off of the support on which it was resting. It fell straight down, and I was directly under it. I put my left arm and hand up to protect myself, catching the beam squarely on my ring finger, breaking the knuckle and the extension bone. I knew that I was in trouble the minute I saw it. One of our hired hands drove Russ Wolfe, J.B. Tankersley, and me to the nearest emergency room, Penrose Hospital, on the north side of Colorado Springs. I panicked on the way to town because I knew what it would mean if the doctor couldn't fix my finger.

The on-duty doctor x-rayed the finger, studied the x-ray for a while, and then called me into his office. "Mr. Humphrey, I can probably set the finger okay, but I doubt that I will be able to bend it much because of the way it broke and how I would have to set it."

My mouth dropped in dismay. "Doctor, I'm an entertainer. I have to be able to play a guitar."

He shook his head in concern.

I had an idea. "Doctor, do you think you could set the finger in a C chord?"

He looked at me askance.

"To play the C chord, the finger needs to be bent a little in a semi-closed position. This position will allow me to play any other chord without a problem." I said a quick prayer.

The doctor stroked his chin in thought. "Let me see what position you want your finger to be in."

I showed him.

"I think I can do that."

He gave me a pain shot, then twisted and turned my finger until he had it in the C position.

He wrapped it up and put a cast on it. "It's done. Good luck with your guitar."

I played the tambourine on stage until the finger healed. When the cast came off, the finger was in perfect position, and everything worked out just fine. I was very thankful. The doctor used to bring other doctors to the show and have me show them the finger that he had set in C. We always had a good laugh about it. One of the guys said that I should insure my fingers, and maybe I should have.

One good thing that came from that near-catastrophe was that after that, Russ wouldn't let any of the musicians work on any project where he might get hurt. To this day, I can't straighten out the finger and probably never will, but I can play the guitar just fine. Fortunately, the finger is bent just enough that I can also hold a golf club without any trouble.

In October of 1975, Russ Wolfe and I decided that we wanted to do something special for the upcoming Bicentennial. Since there were now four Chuckwagons, including the Flying W, Tom Justin's bunch at the Lazy B in Estes Park, Cy Scarborough's Bar D in Durango, Colorado, and Chuck Camp's Triple C in Tucson, Arizona, all of the managers decided to have a reunion show at the Flying W. We also invited Bob Minser to represent the Fall River Chuckwagon, even though it was out of business. Russ Wolfe agreed to take only his food costs out of the price of admission and to split the rest of the money evenly between all of the performers.

The show was a smashing success. This event turned out to be the catalyst for the establishment of The Chuckwagon Association of the West, which still exists today. Now, each year at the end of the season, all of the Chuckwagons in the Association take turns hosting this get-together, and it always sells out. One exception is that Cy likes to do his at the beginning of the season rather than at the end of the season.

In setting up the Chuckwagon Association of the West in October of 1976, the members found that we could pool our buying power to get better prices on food and supplies that we needed in our operations. We also have a set of by-laws, one of which specifies that no alcohol can be served during our regular season. We have since had Chuckwagons apply for membership, some of which we have allowed to join, and some we have not.

One of our requirements is that a Chuckwagon must operate for three years before it can join our

Association. At that time, if a particular Chuckwagon applies, a seasoned member of the Association visits the Chuckwagon and observes how it is run and what kind of a show it has. It's not that we want to limit the number of Chuckwagons in our Association, it's just that we want them to be up to par with what the rest of us do. We are glad to give any advice or help we can to new organizations. We want them to succeed. We want to be sure that when we advertise to our regular customers that there is a new Chuckwagon open, they will not be disappointed. If they are disappointed, we usually hear about it. We want the hot food served hot and the cold food served cold, and we want the entertainment to be western music.

There is a big difference between country music and western music.

One fellow explained the difference this way. "Country music is one feller singing about another feller's wife, and western music is one feller singing about another feller's horse."

That may not be the best explanation, but cowboy music dwells more on the land, the livestock, the lifestyle of the cowboy, and when sung in the Chuckwagon style, the harmony and the yodeling is a big part of the package. This is what our customers expect and what they come to hear, so we try to minimize the surprises.

One hard and fast rule is that the show must be suitable for the whole family. This ties in with the no alcohol rule. We simply cannot advertise a family show and serve alcohol. The first time some guy or gal gets a snoot full and gets loud and obnoxious, the family business is going to leave, and they will tell their friends.

All of the members of the Chuckwagon Association of the West have benefited from group problem-solving. One Chuckwagon may have found a faster method of getting the food served or a more efficient way of cleaning up after the meal. Several of the entertainers, for one reason or another, have performed at more than one Chuckwagon within our Association, and the experience they take with them usually helps any new Chuckwagon at which they might perform.

The mission statement for our Association is as follows:

To consistently provide an authentic western family experience through quality food and entertainment at an extraordinary value.

Last year, 2009, marked the 34th anniversary of the first reunion and was held at the Bar D Chuckwagon in Durango, Colorado. This jamboree has become a destination event for our customers and sells out within just a week or two of the announcement of when and where it will be held.

* * *

It was after that first jamboree in 1975 that I hired Jim Dunham, who had come to work for me at the Lazy B in 1964 right out of college, to work for me at the Flying W Chuckwagon. Jim Dunham had worked for me right out of college and was a real crowd-pleaser with his fast draw demonstrations. He showed different fast draws that were reported to have been used by some of the gunfighters of the old west. He really knew his western history, and he loved to visit with any of the customers who showed an interest, especially someone with knowledge of these western characters.

I remember hearing him debate a fellow one night about whether Butch Cassidy was killed in South America. Jim insisted that he had died there, and the customer was sure that he had come back to the states and died somewhere in the West. About three nights later I heard him debating the same issue with another guest, only this time Jim was on the opposite side of the fence. Both of them seemed to be enjoying the conversation, and we were there to entertain folks. Jim was equally talented entertaining people one-on-one or in groups.

Jim is a specialist in western lore. He worked hard at his fast draw skills and was an asset to the show and a good friend to me. Later on, Jim spent two years with me at the Bar J Chuckwagon in Jackson Hole, Wyoming and then spent several years at the Rocking R in Mesa, Arizona. He currently lives in Cartersville, Georgia, where he is the Director of Special Projects for the Booth Western Art Museum in that city.

Chapter Nine

THE BAR J CHUCKWAGON

My decision to leave the Flying W Chuckwagon in 1963 had been based on several thoughts I had. "I have to try this." "I think I can do this Chuckwagon supper business." "I'm young, and I will try it."

I knew that I needed help at the Lazy B. I couldn't sing all three parts of the music that I knew would be required. I knew nothing about cooking, but I figured that anyone could do that. I knew I could promote a Chuckwagon, and if the show was good enough, it had to be the best, people would come and come again and bring friends

It was my dream to have my own Chuckwagon, and Bob Minser, who left the Flying W with me, had the same dream. We could both hear all the parts of the harmony and agreed that if we could just find someone to sing a good lead, we would be in business. Paul Moyer filled the bill to a tee.

From 1963 to 1967, four short years, Bob, Paul, and I built the Lazy B Chuckwagon and the Fall River Chuckwagon in Estes Park, Colorado, recorded the Montana State Centennial album in Nashville, Tennessee, appeared on the Grand Ole Opry in Nashville, played the Bobby Lord TV show as well as the Tennessee Ernie Ford TV show, had our own TV show on KTVK Channel 3 in Phoenix, Arizona, and rode horseback across the United States from Los Angeles to New York City for the Damon Runyon Cancer Research Foundation. It was a distinguished trio, and we accomplished much in a short period of time.

During all of these years I talked with God. I told Him that we were going to do these things and to please help us along the way. We wanted success in all of these endeavors. As I look back, I had a *give me fame* attitude rather than putting God first in my life and letting Him lead and do the booking for my talent. I have since learned just to let God be in control and let His plan for me take me wherever it is that I'm going. Every prayer now is, *"if it be thy will, Lord,"* and this gives me the calm assurance that whatever I try, it has to be acceptable in His sight or it will fail. I have received more blessings in all areas of my life than anyone will ever know.

* * *

After the ride across the country and after having failed at most of my attempts to be successful, I had a defeatist attitude. Bob, Paul, and I broke up, I declared bankruptcy, my car got repossessed, and I had five kids and a wife for whom I needed to provide food, clothing, and shelter.

As fate would have it, or I should say as God would have it, it was at that time that Russ Wolfe called and offered me a management position, doing what I loved to do and paying me more that I had made in any of the previous four years. You have already read that story. I feel that God impressed upon me the necessity of taking that job, to be patient about having my own business. He told me that I wasn't ready to be on my own yet. I accepted that, and since then, God has been in charge of my life.

* * *

After ten seasons at the Flying W Chuckwagon, Gene Metcalf, an artist who had painted several terrific murals in the winter steakhouse at the Flying W Ranch, approached me early in 1976 with the idea of starting a Chuckwagon supper operation in Jackson Hole, Wyoming. The memories of my two previous attempts at running a strong Chuckwagon business came back to me, and I told Gene that I didn't think I would be interested.

The problem was that the old desire to have my own place returned, and it was on my mind. Gene wouldn't give up on the idea and kept urging me to think about it.

I mentioned the idea in passing to Martha, and you can imagine the reaction that idea elicited from her. She had been through too much in those years while I chased all over the country. She was the one who had stayed home and raised our family, worried about having enough money to pay the bills, took care of all the health issues, and did everything else that goes with raising a family, duties normally shared by two. She had the entire burden on her shoulders and had the patience of Job to stay with me during those years. I thank God that she was the one with our kids during those hard times. She is an angel, and I will always be indebted to her for her tolerance and her love.

Gene kept insisting that I go to Jackson Hole with him just to look at the country and the town and to see if I thought a Chuckwagon would do well in the area. I went, and I fell in love with Jackson Hole.

Now I had convinced myself that there were reasons why I couldn't go to Jackson Hole and open a Chuckwagon. First, I had no money to invest. Second, I had a well-paying job. Third, we had purchased a nice home. Fourth, my family was established, both in school and in our church. Fifth, I already had a place to sing and loved my work.

On the other hand, I still did not own the Flying W, and I wasn't home as much as I wanted to be.

A voice in the back of my mind nagged at me. "You are now ready to start your own Chuckwagon."

I argued with myself. "Should I give all of this up?" "But you have failed before?" "Can I do it this time?"

I prayed long and hard about it and couldn't make up my mind.

Gene hammered away, coaxing me into action. "Babe, I have fifty thousand dollars to put into a new Chuckwagon. We should just do it. Please think about it. And then say yes."

With what I could contribute, we still just had the fifty thousand.

One day, out of the clear blue, I heard a different voice inside. "You are ready to own your own Chuckwagon. This time it will work!"

The next day I called Gene. "I'm ready! Let's do it!"

I knew I could do it somehow with God's help.

The first thing we would need to do would be to find out if there was suitable land available for a Chuckwagon. We made another trip to Jackson Hole for this purpose. After arriving in Jackson Hole, the first place we went was the real estate office of Gene Hoffman.

"I'm sorry, gentlemen. Not much land is available for such an endeavor. The only piece of land that I know of is a half-acre lot along the Snake River." He offered his expert opinion.

"Mr. Hoffman, we need twenty acres. A one-half acre plot is out of the question," I retorted in a bold way.

Mr. Hoffman laughed out loud. "There is no way that that much land can be found anywhere around here for that purpose."

"Do you think that any of the ranchers in the area would part with that much land, Mr. Hoffman." I had to throw something out there.

Mr. Hoffman coughed into his hand. "Real estate speculators and investors have been trying to pry away land in just such a way for years. Few of them have succeeded."

As you may or may not know, Jackson Hole, Wyoming, is located just outside of Teton and Yellowstone National Parks. This is the most beautiful and most visited part of Wyoming. If you have never been to this part of the country, you have missed a place that God spent considerable time and effort creating. One must see it, stand there and gaze at the Teton Range, to understand just how small one really is.

To get to the south gate of Teton and Yellowstone National Parks, you must drive through the town of Jackson. Thousands of tourists visit Jackson Hole every summer, and the town has mostly tourist-oriented businesses situated in close proximity to each other within the city limits. Teton County has very few commercial businesses outside the town of Jackson, and any land that is not National Forest land, Bureau of Land Management land, or owned by the state is privately owned. Only about three percent of the land in the Jackson Hole valley is non-government owned land. This three percent is made up largely of ranches that were homesteaded many years ago. What little is not in ranches is zoned residential. Commercial zoning in the county was very hard to come by.

By then my dream of opening a Chuckwagon in Jackson Hole grew dim, but deep down, I knew that it was going to happen, or we wouldn't be there. The thought came to me that maybe if I talked to a few of the ranchers and explained what I had in mind, I could talk one of them into making some land available to me.

I broached this to Mr. Hoffman, and he just stared at me. "Good luck with that!"

Gene gave me the names of three ranches just the same, the Earl Hardeman Ranch, the Brown Ranch, and the Snake River Ranch.

I called Earl Hardeman first. "Mr. Hardeman, my name is Babe Humphrey. I have a tremendous idea for a western attraction that I believe would do admirably on your ranch. Could we discuss it over a cup of coffee sometime?"

I loved his response. "I've got a pot of coffee on now. Come on over."

In under an hour, we sat in Earl's living room, Gene Metcalf, Earl, Earl's wife, Pat, and I. Our discussion lasted several hours while I explained the what, why, and how come of the business and why I needed an out-of-town ranch atmosphere for this thing to work. I also explained that zoning laws would have to be changed for the parcel of land that the Chuckwagon would be on.

And then I sprang the clincher. "I don't have any money. The only way I can pay you would be a tiny percentage from each meal served during the summer months. You probably wouldn't see much profit for five or six years. It will take the Chuckwagon that long to establish itself.

"I'll need at least twenty acres for buildings, a parking lot, and other attractions to come later. You would have to give me an option to buy the land from you after a certain number of years, if it becomes my desire to do so. This is going to be a success, and I don't want to risk losing it when it is."

Earl didn't fall over dead at these proclamations, so I figured that at least a small part of the battle was won.

The Chuckwagon idea took a bit of time to work out. It wasn't done in one visit by any stretch of the imagination. We all talked about it and hashed it over for several weeks before any decisions were actually made. I'll admit that all of the indecision wasn't on the part of the Hardemans. I had second thoughts, as did Martha, and we discussed it and prayed about it constantly.

Finally, one day Earl called. "Babe, I think that Pat and I would like to give this thing a try. Which twenty acres would you like?"

With Earl's endorsement, Martha and I made our decision. We chose the east end of Earl's ranch, which bordered the road going up to Teton Village. He warned me that we would have to fight for zoning changes. I couldn't believe that Earl had given us a chance.

He knew that Gene and I only had fifty thousand dollars to build a road, a parking lot, a building, pay for permits and surveying costs, and that there would be no up-front money for him. He had no reason to be anywhere near as confident that our project would succeed as I was. After all, he had never been around this kind of thing before and didn't know what to expect.

One day I asked him about it. "Earl, why did you decide to go with me on this?"

He answered me in a straightforward way. "Other land developers and speculators have discussed my land with me and how much money they are going to make for me. When you came to me with your hat in your hand and told me that I wouldn't make much money for five or six years, maybe you were the only one telling me the truth."

The first order of business after tying up the land was to get a zoning change, so we contacted the planning commission. At first I just wanted to feel the members of the planning commission out and get an idea if they would be receptive to my idea. I found out that the commission met every Thursday, unless for some reason they didn't. One time I flew to Jackson Hole from Colorado Springs after getting my name on the commission docket only to find out that one member had decided to go fishing that day. The meeting was cancelled.

After this fiasco, it became obvious that to get anything done, we were going to have to live in Jackson Hole. It was extremely difficult giving notice at the Flying W Chuckwagon. I had been so much a part of the place for ten years that I really hated to go. But go I must if my own dream was to be fulfilled.

Martha and I sold the house, packed, and put stuff in storage. We had to get to Jackson Hole as soon as possible. We needed to be there to get permits, apply for zoning changes, and take care of all of the other things that went into starting a new business.

We finally moved to Jackson Hole in November of 1977. We had three kids still living at home, Scott, Bryan, and Lee Ann, and a dog. All we had to live in was a small motor home that we parked in a campground close to town.

Soon after we arrived in Jackson Hole, we met Stan and Roberta Seaton, who were treasures to us. Stan and Roberta offered us a tiny trailer house in Wilson, next to their home. It wasn't much, but we were thankful to them. It seemed like a mansion to us. It gave us room to spread out. We moved our motor home next to it and used it as an extra bedroom.

Once my family got settled, I got busy working on getting the zoning changed. No one in the Jackson Hole area believed that anyone could run a successful business outside the city limits of Jackson and certainly not one that required folks to drive six whole miles out into the country to have supper and be entertained.

It's a good thing that I believed it and that the little voice inside me kept assuring me that I could do it. If it hadn't been for that inner conviction that we would succeed, I might have bagged the whole thing.

It seemed that one frustration followed another. I tried to keep the whole thing low key, feeling that we would have a better chance of getting approval if we started small and then grew into what I was sure it would become. Gene Metcalf, on the other hand, went about telling everyone what a fabulous operation this was going to be.

I pulled him aside and explained my plan of action, and after thinking about it, he decided that I was right. I sort of told the members of the planning commission that we wanted to feed a few folks and entertain them with some western music and stories. I had one big supporter in Bob Lalonde, who was President of the Chamber of Commerce at the time.

After several months and after jumping through all of the hoops required by the planning commission, I attended yet another planning commission meeting. Two of the commissioners were in favor of my idea, two not so much. One finally said that he would vote for it if I agreed to be open only in the summer. I agreed, and they issued me a Developer's Permit and a Non-Conforming Commercial License. The commission also agreed that I could expand and build on as the business grew. This wasn't too tough to swing, as most of the commissioners didn't think we would last the year out to begin with. A few years later, I went back to the commission and got clearance to operate year around if I wanted to.

The next piece of business on the commission's agenda was to vote on a big new master plan for the valley. If that had passed first, I may not have gotten my go-ahead, so again I sneaked in just under the wire.

The way I looked at it was that the Lord had a hand in how the plan came together. I was really supposed to build this Chuckwagon!

An interesting thing happened while obtaining the building permits after the zoning was changed. I worked to get a building permit that would allow us to serve food that was prepared in our kitchen. Someone from the building department told me that before any permits were issued, we would have to drill a well and have the water tested to make sure that it was safe for human consumption.

Now the site where we were going to build the Chuckwagon was about half a mile back into the trees from the paved road. There was no road to the site, so I applied for a permit to build a road to the site so I could get a well driller in to where the well needed to be.

When I gave my application to the planning commission, a member of the commission told me that the commission wouldn't approve a road until I had my water tested. Now folks, I knew that there were well-educated and smart elected officials on the board and assumed that they would agree that I needed a road to the well site before I could get a rig in to drill the well. Because of this, their response puzzled me. When I asked how I was supposed to have the water tested without a road to get to the water, after a long silence, the members of the commission said that they would have to think about it. A loud, collective peal of laughter resounded in the room from the people assembled there. It goes without saying that I got my road permit.

Stan Seaton had an excavating business, and he volunteered to help. Stan and I, mostly Stan, went to work building a road to the site we had chosen for our main building. The results from the water test came back favorable, so another obstacle was eliminated.

One of my biggest concerns was what I was going to do for entertainers for the show. I had inquired around the valley about singers and guitar pickers and the like and was told of two singers, who were performing at the Stagecoach Bar in Wilson, a small town west of Jackson. Their names were Monte Humann and John Keiser.

I listened to them sing. They sang nice harmony and had sung together for some time. The problem was that they sang country songs, and when I approached them and explained they would have to sing western songs for me, they were a bit apprehensive.

They were, however, interested in the job, so they agreed to try some cowboy songs. I sang a third part to their harmony, and we began with songs like *Cool Water, Tumbling Tumbleweeds*, and a few of the other old favorites. With their knowledge of music, they learned the songs quickly. Thus, the first Bar J Wrangler trio was formed. Doug Barber also joined the group the first year as a singer.

We did not have a place to rehearse, so the Seatons offered us their living room. We sang many a song in that living room, much to the delight of their pet bird, who sang all of the songs with us. I will always be indebted to them for their hospitality and help. I don't know how we would have done it without them.

The trio rehearsed almost every night except on weekends, leaving the daytime hours for drawing up plans for the building and finding someone to build it, meetings with county officials and food suppliers, and designing brochures and getting them printed.

We finally got our building permit in mid-March of 1978 and opened for business in mid-June, just three months later. I had designed the building to be built out of logs and wanted it to be 100 feet long and 67 feet wide with no poles to obstruct the view. I figured we could seat five hundred people in a building this size.

I found a man named Paul Kipp, who had a logging business, and he said that he could build my building for me. We designated the front twenty-five feet to be the kitchen and serving area. The stage occupied the same space as the serving area but was on cables so we could lift it up and out of the way of the serving line. After everybody was served, we lowered the stage back to ground level and did the show.

Left - View of a key-way on the exterior of the building. The inside view is the same. The logs fit in the groove in the center of the key-way extending in both directions.

Bottom - View of three key-ways from the serving porch area on the south side of the building covered by a slanting roof.

We put concrete stabilizers called key-ways at each corner of the restaurant and every twenty-five feet along the sides of the 100 x 67 foot building. These key-ways were made of cement and sunk into the ground six or seven feet with slots on both sides for the logs to fit into. The key-ways held the logs firmly in place and prevented any buckling that might have occurred.

The floor was gravel, and the tables were made out of half logs and weighed over a ton. We had to get a back hoe to move the tables into the building. We found out what the brands of the local ranches were and burned them into the tables to enhance the western décor.

A company in Idaho built the trusses for the roof. This company sent a guy over who got all of the dimensions and then it built the trusses in Idaho. I borrowed Glen Taylor, who offered his truck, to bring the trusses to Jackson Hole. There were five trusses that were welded to the plates on top of the key-ways. Twenty six-foot, twelve-inch logs served as purlins. The builders laid the purlin logs on every four feet running lengthwise, and these were covered with plywood and the plywood with tin roofing. The logs were notched to fit over the trusses and paralleled each other at the ends.

After the building was completed and just before we opened, I found out that I needed a fire permit from the state fire marshal.

He was in Casper, so I made a trip to Casper. I showed the state fire marshal the plans for the building.

"Sir, a building such as this cannot be built. It just isn't feasible. The walls will buckle. It can't be done." The words rolled off his tongue.

I was ready for him. "Would you like to come and look at my building? It's already been built and is ready to open."

The fire marshal indeed came to Jackson Hole to see the building and was surprised by what he saw. I got my fire permit that same day.

Chapter Ten

OPENING NIGHT

Opening night finally arrived in June of 1978, and one hundred twenty people showed up. I think most of them were curious locals who wanted to see what we were doing. We served our basic barbeque beef with all the fixings, barbeque beans, baked potato wrapped in foil, chunky applesauce, hot biscuits with butter and jelly, spice cake, and coffee or lemonade. We served dinner on a tin plate and the drinks in a tin cup, and, of course, it was, and still is, all you can eat.

The new entertainers were nervous, but the show was wildly entertaining, and the audience loved it. We received a standing ovation. What a relief that we had not bombed.

We had a successful opening even though all of the kitchen stoves and other equipment had not come in yet. I think Martha cooked the beans in our trailer and brought them over to the Chuckwagon for serving. Martha, Gene and Paulette Metcalf, and our kids, Jo Anne, who had just moved up to be with us, Lee Ann, Scott, Bryan, and I were the cooks, the clean-up crew, and the dishwashers. All of us had a foot-wetting experience that opening night. We were so relieved and thankful to the Lord to be open and to have had such a successful debut.

Promoting "The Bar-J Chuckwagon" was as high on the list of priorities for us as was eating until money started coming in. I distributed brochures about the Chuckwagon and the show all over the area as I had done at the previous Chuckwagons with which I had been affiliated. This had to be done, but I came up with another way of promoting the business as well as bringing in some income to help out with the grocery bill and other necessities.

I tapped in on my radio background from all of the stations for which I had worked in the past and got a job in 1979 with the local Jackson Hole station, KSGT, on a show named Howdy Partner. The show was broadcast every morning from the world famous Wort Hotel in downtown Jackson Hole. Every morning during breakfast, I wandered around the restaurant, microphone in hand, interviewing out-of-town guests and welcoming them to Jackson Hole. I told jokes and tried to answer any questions guests might have had and tried to make them feel welcome in Jackson Hole. Naturally, the subject of "The Bar-J Chuckwagon" occasionally popped up, and I invited folks and anyone listening to the radio to come out to the show while they were in town. The show was very popular. And then one night the Wort Hotel burned to the ground, taking all of the broadcasting equipment I had stored there with it.

Because the show was so popular, the station bought new equipment, and we moved down the street to the Wagon Wheel restaurant, where we broadcasted for several more years. The show ran primarily during the summer months, Memorial Day through Labor Day.

Eventually, in 1982 we moved the show into the studio, and the format changed. I played old cowboy songs and recited poetry or interviewed an interesting guest who happened to be in town. I had quite a library of the good old cowboy songs by artists such as Roy Rogers, the Jimmy Wakely Trio, the Light Crust Doe

Boys, the Sons Of The Pioneers, Slim Whitman, and recordings from all of the other Chuckwagons in the Association, just to name a few. These were songs that seldom got played on the radio, and I had a good following for this kind of a show.

We had more sponsors than we could handle. I kept the show going until I got so busy at the Bar J that I simply had to cut back.

I still have my library and add to it every chance I get. I still pull out some of the shows that I pre-taped then and listen to them from time to time when I want to re-live some of those good old days. I will always be indebted to KSGT radio for giving me such an opportunity at a time when I really needed it.

In 1979, during our second year at the Bar J Chuckwagon, I met a guy in Wilson who asked me if I had ever heard of building a log building using a Swedish Cope. He told me that he could build such a building. We needed a gift shop, so he built the building we use for our store. The idea of the Swedish Cope is to hollow out the bottom of each log so that it nests on the log that it sits on. This creates a real close fit and eliminates the need for chinking between the logs.

This guy picked out his logs and brought them over to the Bar J, where he let them dry to his liking and then went to work on the store. He scribed each log with an instrument he had, and this is how he got a good fit. That building is as tight a building as you will find anywhere.

One interesting thing he did was come back once a year for three years with a sledge hammer. He went around the building tapping those logs with his sledge, which made the building settle and really snugged it up. After the third year he quit coming, and I haven't seen him since. The next time you're at the Bar J, take a few minutes and observe the workmanship on this building. It is really interesting and impressive.

Things were satisfactory at "The Bar-J Chuckwagon." Over the years, the crowds got larger and larger as the folks around Jackson Hole told the tourists about it. Tourists told other tourists, and the word spread. The Bar J became a popular destination for local folks and tourists alike.

Martha and I both got jobs in the winter time since we put all the profits we could back into the business. I got a job driving a school bus in 1982, and part of my job was to drive the activity bus, which was the bus that took the players to ball games around the state. I enjoyed doing this as our boys were active in sports, and I liked going to the games and being part of the scene.

* * *

Winters in Jackson Hole are harsh, and at times we get a lot of snow, so one of our winter duties is to keep the snow off of the Bar J building. The building has a big roof that catches the snow. One mistake I made when constructing the building was that I should have had it run north and south instead of east and west so the snow would melt off both sides of the building equally. As it is now, the north side is the shady side, and the snow stays on the north side longer than it does on the south side. Most large buildings in Jackson Hole are built running north and south, but it was a detail that I missed, and no one else brought it up. We knew we had a snow problem and kept that roof shoveled off after every large snow storm.

One morning in the winter of 1983, as I was driving out to the main road, I looked at the Bar J building and to my dismay saw that the snow storm the night before had caved the roof in at one corner of the building. My heart sank. I can't tell you how sick I felt when I saw the hole in the roof. What ever would we do? I couldn't even look at the mess that the snow storm had caused. My only thought was that this was a sign that the Chuckwagon was not to be. It was over. All of our work and effort was for nothing. We were finished. We had insurance, but I didn't think it was enough to repair the roof. I was ready to quit.

Now, I said before how I felt that I was supposed to build this Chuckwagon. Again I learned a lesson. A wise man once said, all things happen for a reason. The roof had caved in for a reason, and the Lord hadn't forsaken us at all. Rather, He took my hand and made an adjustment that needed to be made, but until the crisis was over with, I couldn't see this. All I could do was be depressed.

However, this incident made us stronger and more independent and helped us to keep "The Bar-J Chuckwagon" in the Humphrey family.

I told you earlier how Gene Metcalf had convinced me to go to Jackson Hole and open "The Bar-J Chuckwagon" and how Gene's enthusiasm had sparked mine and we got the whole thing going. Gene had good ideas and through his artistic talent had designed brochures, signs, and album covers for our records.

He also assisted with the rest of the advertising. He was a big help in public relations and in other areas that were important to the success of "The Bar-J Chuckwagon".

He and I worked together for four or five years, but Gene's family was in Arizona, where he had other business interests, and the separation from his family was beginning to be a problem for him. He went back and forth to Arizona, however, it just wasn't working out the way he had hoped it would. We had a buy/sell agreement, but I didn't have the money to buy him out. This left us at a stalemate.

It looked like there wasn't going to be anything to buy out, anyway. My son-in-law, Gary Gieck, and Scott and Bryan jumped in, and without much help from me, repaired the building. Gary was a builder and had the skills necessary to do the job. Scott left college for a semester and came home. Bryan, who was in high school at that time, pitched in after school. Somehow they got the roof finished with the money the insurance company had paid. I went to the bank to see if I could get a loan to help with a few extras, and I found out that I could borrow enough to buy out Gene Metcalf's stock in the Bar J.

Gene agreed on the price I could pay and moved back to Phoenix. "The Bar-J Chuckwagon" stayed with the Humphrey family. God does work in mysterious ways. Had the roof not caved in, I wouldn't have realized that I could buy Gene out. I guessed it was meant to be. This re-affirmed for me that we are not in charge of everything that happens in our lives. The Bar J stayed open with His blessing and will continue to stay open as long as it is His will.

When I bought Gene out, I found out that we owned the manufactured home that he had been living in along the road into the Chuckwagon. This got us out of the trailer and into a house and gave us all more breathing room. At last we had room enough to cuss out the dog without getting hair in our mouths.

* * *

Since then, we have poured a cement floor over hot water pipes inside the Chuckwagon so we can keep some heat in the building in the winter to melt the snow. We have also built some reinforcing poles that we put under the roof after we close down in the fall to help support the roof under the heavy Wyoming snow. The building is still turned the wrong way, and we still end up with snow on the north side that has to be hauled away during the winter. The boys made a few engineering adjustments when they repaired the roof to make it stronger, but it has been over twenty-five years, and we haven't had any more trouble with the roof.

While I'm on the subject of the building, we have made a few other alterations too. We added a porch on the south side that we use for our serving line. It is enclosed and out of the weather and the wind. We run four serving lines at once, and this enables us to feed seven hundred or more in less than twenty minutes. Once the new porch was in place, we had room to make our stage permanent. This relieved us from having to raise and lower it every night. Later on, we also extended the back of the building so we could add three more rows of tables. We do have two beams supporting the east end of the building, but because there is just one on each side, they don't obstruct the view of the show. The latest addition to "The Bar-J Chuckwagon" is our covered walkway, where folks can get out of the sun or the rain while they wait to pick up their tickets. We have showcases along each side displaying memorabilia of the Bar J through the years we have operated. We have also put in new restrooms, of which we were in dire need, as our fans have become more numerous and stay longer.

We have always looked for better ways of doing things in the kitchen. We still boil our coffee in thirty-gallon stockpots. We fill size twelve white cotton boot socks with coffee, tie a knot in the top, and throw them in the pot. We haven't been able to figure out a better way of making the amount of coffee we need at one time.

We did come up with a better way to handle the lemonade. In 1982, I got hold of a 500-gallon dairy milk cooler from a dairyman who needed a larger one. I installed it in the attic and ran stainless steel pipes down to the serving area. The dairy cooler keeps the lemonade stirred and cold and perfect.

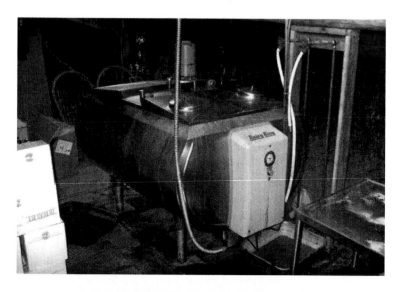

Bryan also came up with an idea several years ago and had potato pots on wheels built that fit right over our gas stoves. When the potatoes are done, we simply roll the potato pots out to the serving line and serve the potatoes from the pots to the plates.

Chapter Eleven

BAR J WRANGLERS

The Bar J continued to grow at a steady pace, and as it grew, various Bar J Wranglers came and went throughout the years, and each one left a footprint on our success.

Some of the exact dates and times are a bit foggy in my memory, but I will try to recall them to the best of my ability. Doug Barber left after the first year and returned to Colorado Springs. We hired Virgil Vapel, a comedy man, who stayed with the Bar J for two or three years. In 1979 we hired a popular fiddle player from New Mexico named Junior Daugherty. J.B. Tankersley, whom I had worked with at the Flying W in Colorado Springs, worked with us for a year in 1980.

I think it was about this time that my son Scott got out of the dishwater long enough to get on stage and sing a comedy song, *He's a Killer*. He was about 16 and still in high school. Collen Campbell played the harmonica for a few years. In 1981, Monte Humann and John Keiser left and were replaced by Scott Vaughn and Dave Sylvester. Dave was an awesome guitar player and was at the Bar J for a number of years, as was Jack McKinsey, a bass player and singer.

I believe that in 1982 Junior Daugherty left and went back to New Mexico. I hired Mark Ralphe from Arkansas, also an impressive fiddle player. Somewhere during these years my son Bryan got up on stage and performed a comedy song called *Foolish Questions*. He was barely out of junior high school.

Bob Loper came along in the eighties. I met Bob sitting around a pot belly stove at Gary Mangus's feed store in the middle of the winter. Gary and I were picking our guitars and singing songs, and Bob strolled in, pulled out his harmonica, and played along. He then sang a song and yodeled another tune.

I just knew that the general public would love to hear him do his thing on stage. So I asked Bob to come to work at the Bar J. He was a bit hesitant about the idea but agreed to give it a whirl. He was with us for several years and added a good deal to our popularity. He was a noteworthy side kick. Bob retired and moved to Cody, Wyoming and is still there. I visit with Bob about once a year, and our Bar J fans ask about him on a regular basis. Bob is also a western artist and has designed the covers of several of our Bar J records and CDs.

Joel Kasserman played guitar for us for a while. Erik Payton replaced Mark Ralphe on fiddle. In 1984 I hired Dean and Russ Eaker. My son Scott joined the Bar J Wranglers about the same time. Scott had just finished college and started singing instead of teaching math. Scott could hear all the parts of the harmony needed in the show. What an asset he was and still is to the Wranglers. Dean and Russ Eaker left in 1985 and were replaced by Mike Whistler on bass and Terry Fields on fiddle.

In 1989 Bryan graduated from college and also joined the Bar J Wranglers. Like Scott, he could hear and sing all the parts of harmony. He brought an incredible yodeling and comedy talent with him as well.

Also in 1989, I happened to be at the Teton County Fair fiddling contest one weekend and listened to all the fiddlers compete for the trophy. One of them stood out way above the others, a young man named Tim Hodgson. Tim had the talent that we needed at the Bar J. Terry Fields had just left, so we needed a fiddle player. I ask Tim if he would be interested. He's been with us ever since. Over the last twenty years, he has also sung high baritone with the Wranglers.

Sometime in the late eighties, we had a special treat at the Bar J. The New York Philharmonic Orchestra was on a tour of the West and came to Jackson Hole to perform at the Teton Village Festival Hall.

The night before the show, the members of the orchestra came to the Bar J. Some of them brought other family with them. We had over five hundred people. These were the best musicians in the world, and we were going to entertain them! I, for one, was awestruck at just the thought of it. I was really worried that they wouldn't like the type of music we sang because it was so different from what they performed. After all, we didn't even have an oboe section.

The busses pulled in and unloaded, and these folks seemed to be pretty much the same kind of people that we had every night. I guess I felt disappointed. I had sort of hoped that this might be our best chance of ever having someone visit the Bar J from Rhode Island, but I didn't see anyone who looked very Rhode Island-ish, so that dream sort of fizzled.

We ran the show as we did every night, and when we finished, the audience stood and applauded like crazy. The conductor came up onto the stage and thanked us for the evening and told us that after we had greeted the crowd and signed our CDs, they had a surprise for us.

After we had spent some time signing CDs, some members of the orchestra played for us. They played *Home On The Range* and several other cowboy songs. After that we all jammed for a while.

The first chair violin player seemed to be the most sociable, and I visited with him for a time. "We were really nervous to be entertaining a group of the best musicians in the world."

He made a confession to me. "It is we who are envious of you. When we play our music, it is all work. We have our heads down reading our music and never get to have eye contact with our audience. We can't relate to our audience as you do. Your Wranglers really have a good time when they perform, and it shows. How I wish we could enjoy our music as you do."

I wanted to tell him that the reason we were not always looking at our music was because none of us could read music, but I thought better of it and just thanked him for his comments. He played a Stradivarius violin that was worth hundreds of thousands of dollars. He let Bob Loper hold it, and Bob still talks about it almost twenty-five years later. The Philharmonic gave us tickets for their show the next night at Teton Village, but, of course, we couldn't go as we had our own show to do, but our wives went and really enjoyed the evening with them.

In the spring of 1990, I received a phone call from a gentleman in Nashville, Tennessee. The producer of a film company there planned to produce a cattle drive program in Red Lodge, Montana staring Roy Rogers, Dale Evans, Randy Travis, Holly Dunn, Denver Pyle, and Dusty Rogers, Roy's son. He told me that Roy wanted the Bar J Wranglers to sing with him and the others. The western songs in the show would be televised on the TNN network. The producer planned to film the show in Red Lodge, Montana in the summer of 1990, probably in July, and we likely would have to be there for several days for filming.

I had a problem with the timing because it was right in the middle of our summer season. We open "The Bar-J Chuckwagon" on June first and serve the meal and do the show seven nights a week through September. That's four months straight through with no time off. We already had several reservations for the summer months, and we just could not close for a few nights at that time of year.

"Thank you for thinking of us, but we will not be able to able to participate because of the timing of your project. We are honored to have been considered." I spoke plainly to the producer of the show.

I felt bad that we could not do it. A chance to sing with Roy Rogers!

A week went by, and I got another call from the producer. "We want the Bar J Wranglers. It will pay you to close that...Chuckwagon thing and come to Red Lodge and sing our songs."

"That would be difficult. We have too many reservations to close during that time. It would cost too much for me to find someone to fill in for us at the Bar J while we're gone."

"Name your price," the producer replied stubbornly.

A high number came out of my mouth.

Without a thought, he played his hand. "No problem. Get it done, and we'll see you in Red Lodge in July."

There were a few folks that I knew of who could entertain at the Bar J, and I thought first of Shelly and Kelly, a husband and wife team. Shelly played the fiddle, and Kelly played the guitar. They knew several western swing songs and had a popular band in the Jackson Hole area. I also contacted Bud and Geri Isaacs. Bud had worked with the Sons Of The Pioneers for a time. Bud and Geri knew all of the western songs and could really sing them, and Geri could also yodel. As luck would have it, both couples said they would love to fill in for us while we filmed in Red Lodge. Bob Christensen, a cowboy poet, who we had worked with on and off for some time, was also available. Bob could entertain with his original poems. With all of these folks, I knew that we could safely leave. Our fans would not be disappointed, and they would be entertained while we were gone.

Everything worked out fine. We filmed the show for several fantastic days and will always remember the time spent singing with Roy Rogers, Dale Evans, and Randy Travis. Randy sang *Cool Water* with us and did a first-rate job. Denver Pyle performed my version of *Drinking From My Saucer*. He had heard the recitation from our Bar J CD and asked if he could do it on the televised show. He did a good job with it. What an experience for the Bar J Wranglers! The show has aired several times on the TNN network since then.

One thing happened during the 1992 season that is worth mentioning. President George H.W. Bush came to Jackson Hole, and the Bar J Wranglers were asked to entertain while he was there. He was to fly into the Jackson Hole airport, give a speech, and then fly right back out again. He planned to stay at Secretary of State Baker's ranch in Boulder, Wyoming and then fly to Jackson Hole in a helicopter that morning. He would only be there for a short time.

The Wranglers and I took the big wagon we used in the Old West Days Parade to the airport and used it for our stage. It was really interesting how the President arrived. For security reasons, there wasn't just one helicopter but several. As the helicopters approached

Bar-J Wranglers
at Redlodge

LR - Byran,
Babe, Scott,
Tim Hodgson,
Bob Loper

LR - Roy Rogers,
Bob Loper,
Bryan Humphrey
with bass, Babe
in chair with
guitar, Tim
Hodgson with
fiddle

LR - Standing
Babe and Bryan,
Sitting - Scott
and Bob, Center
with back turned -
Randy Travis,
Denver Pyle on
stump, Tim
Hodgson with
fiddle

the airport, they conducted some maneuvers, circling and criss-crossing as they flew. They were all identical and all landed in a different area of the runway. After they landed, a jeep convoy drove to one of the helicopters, and President Bush deplaned and got into one of the jeeps along with Secret Service personnel and proceeded to the podium, where he gave his address. After his speech, I had the privilege of meeting him and shaking hands with him. A picture of the handshake hangs in our entry way at the Bar J.

A few years later, in 1993, we were invited to go to Rexburg, Idaho, and perform with the Idaho Symphony Orchestra. The conductor called and wanted copies of our musical scores so that the orchestra could practice our music. I told him that we didn't have anything written down and that the only thing I could do was send him our CDs to listen to. That would have to do, and he took it from there.

To his surprise, we sold the house out, and the crowd loved our performance. We had fun, and I think the Idaho Symphony Orchestra did too. We wore our western clothes just as we do at the Bar J, and the Symphony members were in tuxedos and really looked fabulous. At intermission, we changed into tuxedos, and the members of the orchestra came out in western clothes, complete with wild rags and hats. The audience got a big kick out of that.

While I'm on the subject of shows away from the Bar J, I should mention the time I flew to Orlando, Florida in the winter of 1996 to fill in for Too Slim and became a member of Riders In The Sky for an evening.

One Sunday morning while I was eating breakfast, the phone rang. Doug Green, "Ranger Doug", of Riders In The Sky called. I had met him in Elko, Nevada a couple of years before and had jammed with him throughout the night, so we each had a pretty good idea of what the other could do.

He explained his situation to me. "Too Slim's mother passed away, and he needs to be gone for the funeral. Riders has a show scheduled and tickets sold, and I really don't want to cancel if there is any way around it."

We visited about the show, and Doug and I decided that if they could hold pretty much to just the old standards and that if we could rehearse for an hour before the show, we should be able to pull it off without too much trouble. I would sing the third part of the songs and play the bass.

"I'll be there." I made up my mind to go on the spot.

Plane tickets were bought, and all the arrangements were made. I flew to Denver and immediately found out that my flight to Atlanta was an hour late. When I finally got to Atlanta, the flight to Orlando was two hours late. I could not get to Orlando until 7:30 p.m.

The show was due to start at 7:00 p.m. There went all of our rehearsal time, plus thirty minutes. I had alerted Doug of the problem, and he said to keep on coming. He would take care of details on his end. When the plane arrived in Orlando, I raced off the plane first and sprinted directly to a limousine that Doug had waiting. The limo driver drove as fast as possible to the college auditorium where the show took place. Doug, knowing that I had landed, delayed the concert until I could get there. I jumped out of the limo, grabbed the bass, and stepped right on stage not even taking time to change my clothes. We had to wing the show best we could.

I sang the old Pat Brady comedy song, *He's A Killer*, and sang the harmony for the trio songs. The show went over well in spite of no rehearsal time.

I signed autographs as a member of Riders In The Sky. I will always cherish this memory, and I thank Ranger Doug for having enough confidence in me to ask me to fill in. It just goes to show that in this ride through life, the unexpected sometimes happens, and one has to make the best of it. The show must go on, and you'd better be ready for anything.

*   *   *

The group stayed the same for four years. Scott and I played guitar and sang, Bryan played the bass, and Tim blended in when he wasn't playing the fiddle. Jim Wilson filled in for Tim a couple of times when Tim was gone to the National Old Time Fiddlers Contest at Weiser, Idaho.

During the 1996 season, Bill Camp joined the group. He came to us from the Triple C in Tucson, Arizona. At that time, Scott, Bryan, Tim Hodgson, and I were the Bar J Wranglers. Bill Camp, Chuck Camp's son, had taken over the Triple C when Chuck retired. Since the Triple C was open in the winter time and the Bar J was open in the summer time, Bill asked us to spend winters in Tucson to replace the Sons Of The Pioneers, who had been at the Triple C for years but had left to go to Branson, Missouri.

This all came about in 1995 when Bill Camp called and said that he needed someone to entertain from January through mid-April because the Sons were leaving. We thought it might be a good way to keep busy in the winter. It wasn't a big thing for Martha and me. We could just take the motor home to Tucson for the winter, but it was a different story for the younger guys. They all had families to consider. Bryan had four kids, his son, Michael, his daughter Kylie, and the twins, Kalyn and Kami. Scott had his son, Jake, and daughters, Heather and Emily. Tim had a son, Riley. It was a lot to consider. Tim still taught school in the winter and performed on weekends when we had a show. He would have to make arrangements to become a full time Bar J Wrangler.

We made several trips to Tucson before making the decision to go. We found schools, and the boys decided to buy houses instead of rent. We finally decided that it was doable and agreed to a three-year contract with the Camp family. This included the stipulation that Bill Camp would entertain with us in Jackson Hole as well.

Scott, Bryan, and Tim all bought houses southwest of Tucson, ten or fifteen miles from the Triple

C. Martha and I moved our motor home to the Western Way RV Park, just east of the Triple C. During the three year stint when we worked in both Tucson and Jackson Hole, Scott and Julie gave us another grandson, Clay Humphrey, born May 5, 1997. Tim and his wife also had a daughter, Emma, so the Bar-J family grew by two during this time.

By the end of the three years, moving back and forth and taking kids in and out of schools took its toll. We also got calls from folks wanting us to book shows in the Jackson Hole area, where we could stay year round. These factors helped us decide not to renew our contract with the Triple C. Everyone in the group wanted to go back to Jackson Hole and stay there. We really enjoyed our stint at the Triple C Chuckwagon. We thank the Camp family for giving us the opportunity to make new friends in the Tucson area. Thanks for the memories.

One thing happened one winter while we were in Tucson. We got a call from home that our good friend and benefactor Earl Hardeman had passed away and that the family wanted to hold a memorial service for him at "The Bar-J Chuckwagon".

Earl always loved the Bar J, so it seemed fitting. We made arrangements to fly home and ready the building for the service. It took some doing with snow removal from around the building and the parking lot and getting the building warmed up enough to accommodate those who attended. Earl would have been pleased. You don't find many men now days who will honor a contract with a handshake as Earl did.

* * *

The Bar J has continued to grow throughout the years, and the quality of our singers has improved. Our off-season is getting busier every winter. The demand for our western show away from the Bar J is increasing.

We have performed from Alaska to Florida and most states in between. We have been hired for poetry gatherings, conventions, private parties, bar mitzvahs, and church functions. We have been to the White House, the Walter Reed Hospital, and entertained our wounded troops. We have played in planes, trains, and boats. Tim, our fiddle player, has played at the Orange Bowl. We have played the Dodge National Circuit Rodeo, the National Finals Rodeo, and the Professional Bull Riders Rodeo at Mandalay Bay in Las Vegas, Nevada. We have played at dude ranches, bars, and parks. Apart from when I sang as a member of Riders In The Sky, the current Bar J Wranglers have shared the stage with them and the Sons Of The San Joaquin. I can't count the number of funerals at which we have sung. Our plate is full, and we have been blessed beyond my wildest dreams!

Other entertainers have come and gone during these years. Jim Dunham, whom I talked about earlier in the book, also worked for me at the Bar J, I believe in 1992 and 1993. Bill Camp from the Triple C Chuckwagon in Tucson, Arizona was with us from 1995 to 1998. Terry Humphrey, my nephew, worked for me for a summer. Bob Christensen, cowboy poet, who is helping me with this book, worked with us for a spell. Donnie Cook, whom we call our one man band and plays anything with strings, except a yo yo, is still with us.

Jerry Baxter, formerly of the Bar D Chuck Wagon in Durango, Colorado, sang bass for me for a few years, and what a bass singer he was. He had health problems and eventually had to leave. He was replaced by Danny Rogers from Chugwater, Wyoming, a marvelous western lead and bass singer. He still sings at the Bar J, and we are fortunate to have such a talent on our stage.

I must also mention Don Christensen, who has played keyboard on several recordings with us and plays keyboard for our on-the-road Christmas shows.

Chapter Twelve

THE SHOW MUST GO ON

In October of 1991, I had surgery for an intestine problem. Three years later, in October of 2004, I had a cancer scare and underwent another surgery. We had already booked some shows during this time, and because I was hospitalized, I would, for the first time in over fifty years, have to miss a performance. I knew that the boys were capable of doing the show without me, I just didn't know if they knew that.

Jerry Baxter, who had enjoyed a long career with Cy at the Bar D Chuckwagon in Durango, had come to work for us helping out where needed. On occasion, he announced the show, and we got him on stage for a song each night to show off his deep bass voice, which the audience really liked. He was capable of singing the bass part, so I discussed making a change with my sons, and they reluctantly agreed that it was necessary to make a change. We decided to work Jerry in for the Christmas shows that were coming up and see how it went because I still wasn't one hundred percent.

All of the Wranglers at that time, Scott, Bryan, Tim Hodgson, Donnie Cook, and I, talked about it, and the only decision that made any sense was for them to do the shows without me. They all knew the harmony parts and the flow of the show as well as I did.

The Wranglers did two shows with Jerry. Then they all came to tell me what had happened. When they made their report, I detected a bit of smugness on their part as they told of the standing ovations they had received and of how many CDs they had sold. They seemed pleased at the fact that they had done it without me.

I'm not sure how I reacted to that. On one hand, I was glad that the shows had gone well, but I think it hurt a little that they did such a super job without me. As most of you know, this worked out. We hired Jerry, and away the boys went. They never looked back.

This episode got me to thinking that maybe it was time to slow down and see what else was out there. I had heard folks talk of something called retirement, but I had never paid much attention as I sort of figured that retirement was something for sissies and old folks.

It was hard for me to get off stage, but folks, there comes a time, and I felt that this was it. I still do Christmas shows with the Wranglers and get on stage once in a while and perform a specialty number, but the show is pretty much in their hands now. I am so proud of how well my boys, Scott and Bryan, work together. They have divided up the duties so each is responsible for different areas of the show, and they have things running smoothly.

Scott books shows all over the country in the off season, and business is good. I tell the boys that the show is theirs to run the way they want to as long as I can stop in occasionally and pick up a check.

I really do miss it, but Martha and I thought it was time to do some other things in life. We bought a motor home, but we still spend the summers at the Bar J. Some evenings I go over to the show, and some evenings I don't. We still love it. It is in our blood, and it has been our life for many years.

One venue I really enjoyed and where I am thrilled that we were included was the 2002 Winter Olympics in Park City, Utah. We performed every day that Olympics events were held and got to share our music with folks from all over the world.

During the time that we participated in the National Cowboy Poetry Gathering in Elko, Nevada, we also took part in the Wyoming Cowboy Poetry Gathering in Riverton, Wyoming in all of the years it was held. We have been regulars at the Heber City, Utah Cowboy Poetry Gathering for the past several Novembers and have made friends there. I was presented with the Lifetime Achievement Award at the Heber City Gathering in November of 2004.

On October 2, 2007, the phone rang, and it was a friend and fan of ours, Meg Hauge. She lives in the Washington, D.C. area and spends her summers just up the road on the Snake River Ranch, in which her family has an interest. She wondered if the Bar J Wranglers would be interested in entertaining wounded troops, who were recouping at the Walter Reed Hospital. She wanted to book a few shows on the east coast. The Wranglers were happy to entertain our service men and women at Walter Reed. Meg made all of the

Bar-J Wranglers at Washington D.C.
LR - Scott, Bryan, VP Dick Cheney, Pres. George Bush, Tim Hodgson, Danny Rogers, Donnie Cook

arrangements and also served as host and guide for the Wranglers while they were there. She took them all around and showed them the sites, which also included a tour of the White House. While at the White House, they were invited into the Oval Office by President Bush and Vice President Dick Cheney. They enjoyed a casual conversation with the leaders of our nation. This was a totally unexpected surprise for them. Danny Rogers, our bass singer, was really impressed as it was his first road trip with the Bar J Wranglers.

He asked, "Is this a great job or what?"

The 2007 trip was a success, and I wished I could have been with them. As fate would have it, however, in 2008, the phone rang again. Meg invited the Wranglers back to Walter Reed. This time I was invited too. In addition to the Walter Reed Hospital, we performed at the Library of Congress and the John F. Kennedy Center for the Performing Arts.

We were invited by a friend of ours, Danny Rodgers, no relation to our bass singer, to go to Richmond, Virginia and entertain for a gala event he sponsored. He works for the Department of Defense designing new weapons for the Marine Corps. He planned to introduce a new invention to some Generals and other dignitaries. The invention would not only benefit the military but also the general public. He had been given permission to sell stock to the public, and this was the kick-off party for that promotion. We performed along with a few other entertainers and had a fantastic time doing it.

We also entertained at a Veterans Administration hospital in that area and had a chance to say thanks to our wounded troops who were there. Before we left, we took a ride in old World War I and World War II aircrafts that Danny had collected over the years. I went up in an old World War I bi-plane, which was fun. Some of the others rode in a helicopter he had bought for use in the new invention he had developed. What a time we had!

The entire trip was terrific. We met new people and made new friends and fans for the Bar J. It is one of the things I will never forget.

Another 2007 phone call I received led me down a trail I had never thought about riding. Now, I had not heard of VeggieTales. It turns out that VeggieTales is a Christian based DVD series for children distributed all over the world. Bible stories are acted out by vegetable cartoon characters. These DVDs are shown on television and are used at home and in Sunday School classes and are excellent entertainment for the young and the young at heart. Besides that, they tell a Bible story and impart a moral message.

The phone call came from Brian Roberts, who was the producer for VeggieTales. He got my number from Scott, who suggested that he call me. He had approached Scott to see if he could get the Bar J Wranglers to do the music on an upcoming production called *Moe and the Big Exit*. He was doing the story of Moses, and he wanted to do it in a western setting, one that depicted the children of Israel as zucchinis digging out the Grand Canyon in Egypt rather than building pyramids. Scott told Brian that the timing was bad. Brian had indicated to Scott that the Wranglers would be needed in Nashville during the summer months.

Brian also told Scott that he needed a narrator who could tell the story in a western voice. Brian told me that he had called my home and when he heard me on my answering machine, he knew that my voice was the voice he wanted to use for his production. He asked if I would be interested in coming to Nashville for recording and if it would be all right if he sent some songs and a script to me so he could conduct an audition over the phone with the music director, Kurt

Heineken, and the story writers, Mike Newark and Phil Viscera.

I agreed to take a look, and the next morning I had the material on my door step, it having come via UPS. In the meantime, I quizzed my grandkids about VeggieTales and found them to be shocked that I knew so little about such a big part of their lives. I found out that they all had a nice collection of VeggieTales, so I decided that this wasn't just one of my friends seeing if he could win a bet that he could get me to talk like a cucumber.

I looked at the material and read the letter asking me to get familiar with the script and go over the songs and be prepared to do an audition over the phone in about four days. I waited for the audition with the writers and the producers. The phone call came.

"Say, fellas. I like the songs, but I don't think they have the western flavor that they need. They are also in the wrong key for me. I have worked them over a bit. I hope that's all right." I felt compelled to honesty.

The music producer asked me to sing the songs the way I thought they should be sung. I played my guitar and sang the songs, and the writers and producers really liked what I had done with them. They seemed excited. Kurt said that he would re-write the arrangements for me.

The script reading was interesting, to say the least. First, I had to read the script sounding cheerful, then I read it sounding sad, changing the mood of the story throughout the audition. The producers later explained that they wanted me to audition in that way so they could find out if I was producible and could follow their directions. All of them seemed happy with the audition, and before long I had plane tickets to Nashville and reservations at a hotel near the VeggieTales studios.

As I said, the name of the DVD is *Moe and the Big Exit*. You will see Moses dressed like a cowboy leading his people out of bondage in Egypt. I am a singing carrot. Dressed as a cowboy, I sing and narrate the story. I enjoyed this opportunity to be a witness for God in telling this story to children immensely. I hope you all pick up this DVD and enjoy watching it as much I enjoyed performing on it.

* * *

Before I forget, I want to thank the communities of Jackson Hole for the support they have given us and for the recognition they have bestowed upon us. We have a whole wall of plaques in our entry way from various organizations acknowledging us for some of our accomplishments. We hope that we are deserving of the honors given to us. We won the Beef Backer of the year award in 1994. This award recognized us for selling fifty thousand pounds of beef and for being the largest user of beef in Wyoming. There are too many to mention, but another one I am proud of is being named Business Person of the Year in 1997. We've never received an award for it, but our Chuckwagons of the West Association was told that it is the biggest user of pinto beans in the country.

Next time you come out to the Bar J, take the time to walk down our Hall of Fame entrance in the ticket area to see the plaques, trophies, pictures, and other things we have on display. Also take a look in the show area. You might get a kick out of it. At least you will have your memory jogged.

Several items of interest that you may want to look for can be found in the main building. On the south wall at the back you will see a lady's red dress. This dress was given to us the first year we were in operation by some folks from Kansas. It had special meaning to them, and they asked us if we would like to put it on display. We have had it ever since. See if you can spot the hand-carved train that sits on one of the ceiling beams. This train was carved by Martha's uncle, Boots West, with a pocket knife. It is a piece of work.

On the stage is my grandfather Humphrey's anvil, one that came from Missouri all those years ago when my grandfather first moved to Colorado. There's a saddle from the Brown Ranch here in Jackson Hole, and in the gift shop we have a vest, chaps, and a sweat-stained hat worn by Martha's father, Ed West.

You may wonder about all the boots hanging from the ceiling. We invited any of the locals who had some old boots to bring them to us so we could hang them up. One of the pairs of boots that Tony Llama gave me for the Great Trek hangs about a third of the way back on the south side. Currently Bryan is hanging up some old hats that our patrons have brought in.

Views inside The Bar-J

We've gathered a ton of memorabilia and a million memories over the years. I've tried to recall these memories to the best of my ability, but I am certain that after this book goes to print, I will remember other things that happened along the way and will wonder how I could have neglected to include them.

* * *

The shows are getting better, the harmonies tighter, and it is amazing how well the boys are doing without me. I just wonder how far they can go if I get out of the way. Indeed, they are now "The Bar-J Chuckwagon". I am enjoying every minute of their success.

Our five children have given us nineteen grandchildren. It seems as though they all came at once. It is a pleasure watching them grow. At the time of this writing, some are still in high school, some are in college, and some are married. In fact, we now have four great-grandchildren. Sadly for us, God has taken two of our grandchildren. Jessica Humphrey, Scott's first born, and Cody Shervin, Jo Anne's third son. We miss them both but know we will see them again in heaven one sweet day.

LR - Diane, Lee Ann, Martha, Babe, Jo Anne, Bryan, Scott

We've gone from zero to seventy-five years in just a few pages, so I'm sure we didn't get it all. I've shared mostly the good times and left out most of the bad times. I've done things that I'm proud of and a few things that I'm not so proud of, but I'm sure that every life has in it both some good rides and some bad rides. I thank God every day for His amazing grace and ask Him to guide me on my life's journey.

As I've said before, I'm a lucky man. I've been able to live my dream and enjoy the benefits of that dream. My wish for all of you is that you too have a dream and that you realize joy while living it. As you travel along the trail of life, my advice would be to take the good Lord with you. He will make all the difference in the world.

As for me and my ride, I've been blessed and have loved every minute of it!

Acknowledgements

Most of the folks that I have mentioned who have helped "The Bar-J Chuckwagon" become what it is today have been performers. There is, however, a long list of people who have had a hand in our success who have never been on stage.

For several years, my mother and her sister, Alta, spent the summer in Jackson Hole helping with the preparation and the serving of the food. Chad Hansen, who was a good friend and college classmate of Bryan's, spent many summers washing dishes and keeping the back end in order. Scott's wife, Julie, has been our accountant for years, doing all of the bookwork that is necessary for a business of this nature. She handles our payroll, pays our bills, and sees to it that the stores are stocked with merchandise. She probably puts in more hours than anyone else in the organization, and we couldn't operate without her. Bryan's wife, Sandy, has always helped in any aspect of the business where I needed her, working in the kitchen, selling tickets, serving, or cleaning,

The tradition of Bar J Chuckwagon

An evening of song and supper with the Humphrey family

By Peg Kirk

These days, the term "chuckwagon" may conjure up an image of people dressed like cowboys, eating beans around a fire and trying to act "Western." But Babe Humphrey puts those connotations to rest at Bar J Chuckwagon, where the spirit of the old West is alive and surprisingly enough, real.

Real wranglers, real coffee and real Western accents are part of the Bar J tradition. Apparently it works, for by summer's end approximately 50,000 people will have visited the Chuckwagon, many of them repeat customers.

Now in its eleventh year of business, the Bar J is owned and operated by the Humphrey family. Babe Humphrey and his wife, sons, daughters-in-law and aunts, along with eight other employees, perform the duties required to feed and entertain over 500 people each evening. Some cook, some serve, some sing, some do all; there's a job for everyone and everyone does it with a genuine smile.

But it takes more than a smile to feed over 500 people in less than 20 minutes, and the Humphrey family does it seven days a week all summer long. In the words of one employee, "we've got it down to a science."

It is the science of knowing what people want, and giving just that. According to Babe, Bar J's success is due to the fact that it is unique to the West, a Western experience that can't be found elsewhere.

"People come here to see the West, not to see the same places they would have back home," Babe said. "We

want to give them the West, what it was and what it is now."

And so visitors to Bar J get a feel for the cattle driving days when cowboys ate and sang around the chuckwagon. A hearty meal of barbequed beef, beans, baked potato, applesauce and biscuits is served up on tin plates. Babe explained that the food is as close to an authentic chuckwagon meal as possible.

Especially interesting is the coffee, made by throwing a actual sock full of coffee grounds into a huge pot of boiling water. This is cowboy coffee, served steaming in a tin cup with a view of the Tetons just beyond. Drink this and you'll be listening for the cattle.

After supper, the Bar J Wranglers take the stage for an hour of songs stories and bantering. Headed by Babe on his guitar, the Wranglers play some great old Western music complete with yodeling, harmonica and fiddle. In front of a crowd of many music generations, the Wranglers are able to fill the gaps

and bring the house down with the "Orange Blossom Special."

With so much going for it, it's the simple things that make Bar J unique. Second helpings are encouraged, wranglers walk around filling coffee cups, Babe visits with people before supper. The atmosphere is comfortable and the staff is genuine.

"We come to Bar J every year," said one couple from Cody. "It's good food, good music, and good company."

Bar J Chuckwagon is located on Teton Village Road. The price for dinner and entertainment is $9 for adults and $3.50 for children. Reservations are recommended. For further information, call 733-3370.

Charlie Mathis, the chuckwagon cookie, prepares biscuits range-style, cooking them under piles of hot coals.

In the late eighties, Charlie Mathis was a fixture as our first Dutch oven cook. He cooked biscuits outside over hot coal fires in Dutch ovens while he visited with the crowd. For years, Rondo Olsen served faithfully as a greeter and was known by sight by our regular customers. Forty Ford and his wife, Mary Anne, helped out for several years. Some of you will remember Forty getting up on stage and doing a little soft shoe dance from time to time. He, like Mr. Olson, has now passed on, and we miss them both.

Others I want to remember include Hyrum and Vita Auger, Neil and Verna Darrington, Ron and Jody Henson, Jackie and Lynn Jacob, Donna and Gary Broughton, and Martha's parents, Ed and Alice West, who helped in the early stages of the Bar J. All of these folks went beyond the job they were paid for and gave the Bar J much more than we expected them to.

I also want to thank the wives of the Wranglers, who have helped out in the gift shops or in the serving line or anywhere else they were needed. I know I will think of others that I have failed to mention as times goes by, and I want them to know that it was not intentional if anyone got left out.

I give thanks to God that He allowed "The Bar-J Chuckwagon" to flourish. I also want to thank my family, for without their help, the Bar J wouldn't be. "The Bar-J Chuckwagon" was my dream, not theirs. I thank them for making it possible for me to live my dream.

Each of our five kids means so much to me that it is hard to put into words. Diane, Jo Anne, and Lee Ann are each in her own way making this world a better place to live in. I am proud of who they are. Scott and Bryan are now running the Bar J and have raised the bar, so to speak. I especially want to thank my wife Martha, who, as I said, has to be a special angel for sticking with me along the way.

Finally, in closing, I want to thank you folks who are reading this book and all of our fans, wherever they may be. Without your support, the Bar J would not be the success that it is. Come up and see us whenever you can get away.

Entertainers at "The Bar-J Chuckwagon" by year

1978 – Babe Humphrey, Monte Humann, John Keiser, Doug Barber

1979 – Babe Humphrey, Monte Humann, John Keiser, Virgil Vapel, Junior Daughtery

1980 – Babe Humphrey, Monte Humann, John Keiser, Virgil Vapel, Collen Campbell

1981 – Babe Humphrey, Virgil Vapel, Collen Campbell, Scott Vaughn, Dave Sylvester

1982 – Babe Humphrey, Collen Campbell, Dave Sylvester, Bob Loper, Jack McKinsey, Mark Ralphe, Scott Vaughn

1983 – Babe Humphrey, Collen Campbell, Dave Sylvester, Bob Loper, Jack McKinsey, Scott Vaughn, Joel Casserman

1984 – Babe Humphrey, Dave Sylvester, Jack McKinsey, Bob Loper, Mark Ralphe

1985 – Babe Humphrey, Dave Sylvester, Bob Loper, Dean Eaker, Russ Eaker

1986 – Babe Humphrey, Bob Loper, Dean Eaker, Russ Eaker, Scott Humphrey

1987 – Babe Humphrey, Bob Loper, Scott Humphrey, Mike Whistler, Erik Payton, Mark Ralphe

1988 – Babe Humphrey, Bob Loper, Scott Humphrey, Mike Whistler, Terry Fields

1989 - Babe Humphrey, Bob Loper, Scott Humphrey, Bryan Humphrey, Terry Humphrey, Tim Hodgson

1990 – Babe Humphrey, Bob Loper, Scott Humphrey, Bryan Humphrey, Tim Hodgson,

1991 – Babe Humphrey, Scott Humphrey, Bryan Humphrey, Tim Hodgson

1992 – Babe Humphrey, Scott Humphrey, Bryan Humphrey, Tim Hodgson, Jim Dunham, Bob Christensen

1993 – Babe Humphrey, Scott Humphrey, Bryan Humphrey, Tim Hodgson, Jim Dunham, (Jim Wilson, one week for Tim while gone to National Fiddle Championship)

1994 – Babe Humphrey, Scott Humphrey, Bryan Humphrey, Tim Hodgson

1995 – Babe Humphrey, Scott Humphrey, Bryan Humphrey, Tim Hodgson

1996 – Babe Humphrey, Scott Humphrey, Bryan Humphrey, Bill Camp, Tim Hodgson

1997 – Babe Humphrey, Scott Humphrey, Bryan Humphrey, Bill Camp, Tim Hodgson

1998 – Babe Humphrey, Scott Humphrey, Bryan Humphrey, Bill Camp, Tim Hodgson

1999 – Babe Humphrey, Scott Humphrey, Bryan Humphrey, Tim Hodgson, Donnie Cook

2000 – Babe Humphrey, Scott Humphrey, Bryan Humphrey, Tim Hodgson, Donnie Cook, Jerry Baxter

2001 – Babe Humphrey, Scott Humphrey, Bryan Humphrey, Tim Hodgson, Donnie Cook, Jerry Baxter

2002 – Scott Humphrey, Bryan Humphrey, Tim Hodgson, Donnie Cook, Jerry Baxter

2003 – Scott Humphrey, Bryan Humphrey, Tim Hodgson, Donnie Cook, Jerry Baxter

2004 – Scott Humphrey, Bryan Humphrey, Tim Hodgson, Donnie Cook, Jerry Baxter

2005 – Scott Humphrey, Bryan Humphrey, Tim Hodgson, Donnie Cook, Jerry Baxter

2006 – Scott Humphrey, Bryan Humphrey, Tim Hodgson, Donnie Cook, Jerry Baxter

2007 – Scott Humphrey, Bryan Humphrey, Tim Hodgson, Donnie Cook, Danny Rogers

2008 – Scott Humphrey, Bryan Humphrey, Tim Hodgson, Donnie Cook, Danny Rogers

2009 – Scott Humphrey, Bryan Humphrey, Tim Hodgson, Donnie Cook, Danny Rogers

2010 – Scott Humphrey, Bryan Humphrey, Tim Hodgson, Donnie Cook, Danny Rogers

Martin D-18, Made in 1969
Lots of Pearl, Bought from
Singing Sam for $200.^{00}

Martin D-18, Made in 1953
This guitar went on the Great
Trek Coast to Coast Horse
Back Ride in 1966

Super 400 Gibson - Made in 1951
Was a birthday present from the
family, and was used in the
Sammy Davis Jr. Band

Gallagher Guitar
Made in 1985
Doc Watson Model

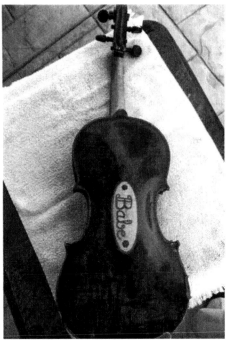

Grandpa's Fiddle
My name was put on the back by Hyrum Auger
Who worked at The Bar-J

Index of people and places along the ride.